Pastoral Counseling

with People in Distress

Harold J. Haas

CONCORDIA PUBLISHING HOUSE

Concordia Publishing House, St. Louis, Missouri
Concordia Publishing House Ltd., London, E. C. 1
© 1970 Concordia Publishing House
Library of Congress Catalog Card No. 77-99316

To my parents

Clergymen are busy people, and not the least of the things they are busy about is helping people in distress. Their activities in this area range from troubleshooting and patchwork to prolonged counseling relationships. The range of their sophistication (in the good sense) about approaches to pastoral care and counseling varies greatly. Many, it seems, struggle with a sense of inadequate training in the area of mental and emotional problems. What they need, in my opinion, is a point of view about how to meet people in trouble and a reasonably concrete set of ideas about the methods they can use in counseling. They also need some signposts that will tell them when a problem is beyond their competency so they can make appropriate referrals to other members of the mental health team. I have tried to meet those needs in this volume. Basically I have tried to put together my knowledge of the pastoral ministry and my knowledge from clinical psychology to produce a point of view about how to approach people in distress and a way to approach counseling. I have also drawn a distinction between pastoral *counseling* and pastoral *care*.

I want at this point to enter a disclaimer. I have not attempted to develop here a theology of pastoral counseling and care. That is a monumental task, which requires a separate volume entirely. I have assumed that the pastor who reads this book is deeply immersed in his own theology. I have 7 seen my task as one of presenting him with a point of view about counseling and human interaction that he can reject, borrow from, or integrate with his theology as he sees fit. At the end are further suggested readings in the secular literature on counseling and psychotherapy.

I am indebted to many people who have contributed to my thinking over the years, and to many persons who entrusted themselves to my counseling efforts and from whom I learned much. Among my professors, I wish particularly to acknowledge my indebtedness to Dr. Marvin J. Feldman at (what was then) the University of Buffalo and to Dr. Carl N. Zimet at the University of Colorado Medical Center. I wish to express deep gratitude for many stimulating conversations to my close friend and colleague, Dr. Martin L. Maehr, now at the University of Illinois, and to Miss Margaret Hermes of the Concordia Senior College faculty for much patient help and advice in the preparation of the manuscript.

HAROLD I. HAAS
Fort Wayne, Indiana

Contents

1

Distress

Mr. Smith works in a factory. He has a wife and two cute little girls. He's worried because the assembly line he works on may be shut down, and he may be laid off. He has bills to pay and obligations to meet. Some nights he can't sleep.

Mr. Cooper is a middle-aged salesman. He has had persistent stomach pains for nearly 6 months. He fears going to the doctor because of what the doctor may tell him.

Stan is 17. He has a severe case of acne. He spends most of his time away from people, reading and daydreaming. Stan hasn't had a date since he was a freshman in high school, because he is so self-conscious.

Charlie S. drinks!

Mary Beth, 26, is becoming progressively quieter. Her mother worries because Mary Beth seems to be losing interest in life. Her mother is so close to her that she doesn't see the little peculiarities that have slipped into Mary's behavior in the past 2 years.

Benjamin Black, M. D., is miserable. And his son Jim is miserable. After 3 years of college, Jim knows he doesn't want to follow in his father's footsteps in medicine. Yet his father insists on it. Every discussion ends in anger and harsh words.

The Youngs have a mentally retarded child. They refuse to admit the fact, but deep inside they know it's true. They dread the day when they will have to face the problem openly. *11*

The widowed Martha Johnson still doesn't fully realize her husband, Peter, is gone. Somehow it is all a bad dream. Sometimes she thinks: "Soon I will wake up, and everything will be right again."

All these people, and in many cases their family and friends too, are experiencing distress. For some of them the distress is mild. Unless someone called their attention to it, they might not recognize it. For others the distress is acute and painful. They know well that something hurts, although they may not know why. Between the extremes are every shade and degree of discomfort.

The Nature and Scope of Distress

The term *distress* covers a wide variety of emotional reactions. It refers to the feeling of *anger* that can make a man tremble. It refers to the *anxiety* that flutters at the edge of awareness and to the *fear* that makes a child run all the way home in the dark. Distress includes the *grief* that accompanies loss, the *pain* of a physical or psychological injury, the *remorse* that follows cruelty. *Fear, shame, guilt, disgust, jealousy, envy, hate, loneliness* are all types of distress. We easily recognize the negative quality of these emotions, for they all imply discomfort or malaise. No one hesitates to call them unpleasant.

Feelings of distress lead people to call for the pastor's help. People seek help in the grief of death, the anxiety of illness, the pain of injury. Although they may not always seek it, people need help to deal with feelings of loneliness, shame, guilt, depression, fear, and many other emotional reactions. And they need help in dealing with the situations that give rise to these emotions.

The concept of distress implies that there are not only varieties but degrees of distress. Distress can be mild or intense, nearly absent or acute. For example, the anxiety of impending surgery may be slight when the operation is still 3 weeks away. It may increase perceptibly when the patient enters the hospital. And it may reach the stage of panic when they start wheeling him to the operating room, if he has not been adequately sedated. The distress a person experiences as feelings of guilt may be slight — as in the case of a man who cheats on his income tax and rationalizes that the government has gotten too big and wasteful. But guilt feelings can be extremely intense — as in the case of a woman who can't forget her premarital sexual indiscretions.

The degree of distress a person experiences changes from day to day, and even from moment to moment. But long-term trends also occur. Some people find themselves relatively distress-free during substantial portions of their lives. They have ups and downs, but the overall picture reveals an absence of severe or prolonged distress. Other people are chronically distressed for years. Their degree of distress fluctuates too, but it ranges from moderate to severe. These people might be technically thought of as emotionally disturbed in a psychiatric sense, and yet the majority of them live with their distress. They never get near a psychiatrist's office or a psychological clinic. The pastor can often render a distinct service to them.

Distress, therefore, is not something a person has or does not have. Everyone experiences emotional distress to some degree. Most people experience it to a mild or moderate degree with considerable frequency. At least a few episodes of severe distress occur in every person's life. Emotional distress occurs much more commonly than most people realize, because in our society we teach people to keep their feelings to themselves. We lead them to think that showing fear or anger or grief is a sign of weakness. Christians may even be told that such emotions show a sign of weak faith. But the picture one gets as he views the panorama of human distress is that most people are distressed some of the time, some people are distressed most of the time, and a few people are distressed just about all the time.

It may seem contradictory to say so, but people do not always feel their distress directly. This is because some distress gets transformed into other symptoms — for example, physical illnesses. Disorders like ulcers, chronic headaches, high blood pressure, indigestion, sexual impotence, and even fatigue can be the result of unconscious emotional conflicts. In other instances the distress, the conflict, expresses itself through actions and is felt only minimally or not at all by the person. For instance, alcoholism, juvenile delinquency, chronic irresponsibility, and sexual perversions also reflect conflicts, often with little conscious feeling of personal distress. However, we cannot always know just how much subjective discomfort the person really feels. People often try to deny that there is anything wrong with them.

Distress and Mental Disorder

The last paragraph raises the question of the relation between distress and mental disorder. Emotional distress and mental disorder aren't the same thing. In order to properly differentiate them, we need a definition of mental disorder. Unfortunately, no brief and unambiguous definition of mental disorder exists. The term *mental disorder* covers a most diverse range of phenomena in human thoughts, feelings, and actions. Briefly but somewhat inadequately put, mental disorder refers to conditions that (1) seriously incapacitate a person for carrying out his ordinary life role or (2) make the person dangerous to himself or to others or (3) leave him so severely distressed and uncomfortable or make those around him so distressed and uncomfortable that professional help is needed. Such a definition clearly overlaps with the concept of distress we are using, and the point where a person requires referral to another mental health professional is not easy to establish. (In Chapter 7 we take up the signs of severe disorder and the topic of referral.)

Obviously then, emotional distress covers a broader range than mental disorder. Distress refers to the whole gamut of emotional discomfort, from mild unpleasantness to the most severe and disturbing emotional experiences. Distress does not necessarily imply abnormality. Indeed, under some conditions, not to experience emotional distress constitutes abnormality. For example, not to have some feelings of guilt or regret when one has injured another person is abnormal. Not to feel grief at the death of a close relative or friend is atypical. Thus while we find emotional distress present in most but not all mental disorder, mental disorder is diagnosed in only a percentage of emotionally distressed people. How big a percentage is difficult if not impossible to say.

Emotional distress and mental disorder meet at two important points, however. When emotional distress is highly unrealistic or inappropriate, it reaches the point where terms like *abnormal* and *mental disorder* are usually used. For example, the woman who becomes hysterical at the loss of a small amount of money or a broken dish demonstrates the kind of behavior that might be judged unrealistic. If such reactions occur frequently, they might be taken as evidence of a mental disorder, possibly a neurosis. Second, when emotional distress prevents the individual from carrying on his usual life activities, such as going to work, sleeping properly, enjoying social relations, it reaches the point where mental disorder is also frequently diagnosed. Thus *incapacitation* is always taken as a serious symptom.

Nonetheless, a great deal of latitude must be allowed. Many people have highly unrealistic emotional reactions, and many people are temporarily incapacitated by emotional distress who are never diagnosed as mentally disturbed.

There was a time when such people were viewed simply as undetected cases of mental disorder. More recently, mental health professionals have begun to ask about the appropriateness of such a view. There is a growing awareness that many people manage to carry on even though they are emotionally distressed a good proportion of the time. There has been a shift away from labeling such people with the terminology of mental disorder. Among such people we find some of the most creative, the most socially acceptable, and the most valuable members of society. They number in their midst doctors, lawyers, ministers, teachers, students, housewives, businessmen — in fact, every type of human being. The present trend treats as mentally disturbed only those people who are dangerous to themselves or to others, or who cannot care for themselves, or who seek specialized help.

The Causes of Distress

Before proceeding to a discussion of the possible physical and psychological causes of emotional distress, we want to develop the idea of the person as a *perceiver*. Some characteristics of human *thinking* also require examination.

Perceiving and Thinking

Without taking too mechanical a view of man, one can conceive of a human being as an organism (the psychologist's favorite word for a person) that is constantly receiving and carrying on transactions with a large input of information. This information comes from without in the form of sounds, sights, tastes, smells, skin sensations. It comes equally from within, from muscle sensations, pains, tickling, a feeling of fullness in the stomach. Some of it comes in small quantities — a pinprick or a flash of light. Some comes in large quantities — a 10-minute conversation, a 2-hour movie. Some of it is disorganized — noise. Some of it is organized — music. Some of the information permits quick interpretation, like the pain of a toothache. Some of it is nearly meaningless, like a babble of children's voices or an unusual odor. Some of the information is generated by things—a picture, the aroma of fresh-baked pie. Some of it is generated by oneself or other people—memories of home, a person calling your name. Some of the information coming to the organism is not strong enough to be detected, and the person doesn't react to it, like a faint light or a distant voice. Some of the information is received and dealt with at a purely physio-logical level—the muscle fatigue from sitting too long that makes us shift our position, the drop in loudness of a person's voice that, without our knowing it, causes us to lean forward and listen more intently. Some of the information receives a quick interpretation and is forgotten—"That's John coming in the back door." Some gets prolonged attention—"What did she mean by that remark?"

Three aspects of this perceiving activity are particularly important from the point of view of emotional distress. One, a human being does not merely receive information, nor is human behavior merely reactive. A person seeks, organizes, interprets, and makes value judgments about this information. Information-yielding events not only happen to him, he seeks them out, he *makes* them happen. And when they have hap-pened, he evaluates them as good, bad, nice, naughty, im-portant, unimportant, beautiful, ugly, painful, or pleasant. Thus man both initiates events that cause him emotional distress and may be their victim. But by ignoring them, not seeking them out, or interpreting them differently, a person can alter or be helped *through counseling* to alter the events that cause him emotional distress. The housewife can stop trading at the store that leaves her annoyed and frustrated every time she shops. The thrice-divorced woman can stop getting entangled in bad marriages. The insecure adolescent can interpret the refused date realistically—"The young lady already has a boyfriend" — and not as a blow to his self-esteem.

A second important aspect of this perceiving activity lies in the fact that man can hold in focus the information coming to him. He can keep it in awareness in the form of *thoughts* for brief periods of time. Through a neurological event in the brain that is only partly understood scientifically, the individual has a representation of the original source of information available. Thus the words linger briefly; the sight stays in the mind of the beholder. But even more important, a substantial portion of this information is available on demand as a *memory*. Memories are new neurological events with respect to time, but they are approximate reinstatements of the old events with respect to similarity. Actually memories are indistinguishable from thoughts from our point of view, and it is this human ability to briefly hold or reinstate information-yielding events that makes emotional distress possible. For example, if the pain of the hypodermic needle was not in some way retained, the word *needle* could produce no reaction in the child. If the words and caresses of a loved one could not be held in mind for a moment, it would be impossible to feel elation that she loves. If one could not recall the thoughts and feelings in which lust is embodied, there could be no possibility of feeling guilty. This perceiving and thinking activity goes on continuously and contiguously. That is, one perception with its attendant thoughts blends into the next, and thoughts and memories follow one another in continuous stream.

The third important aspect of the perceiving and thinking activity is that thoughts and memories are perceivable just as any other event is perceivable. And like other perceptual events, thoughts and memories yield information that can be held in focus or reinstated at some later time. This makes it possible to have emotional reactions to thoughts themselves.

One can feel pleased as he recalls a nostalgic scene from youth. He may feel mildly distressed as he recalls the embarrassment of not being able to remember a friend's name. He can feel intensely distressed, to the point of panic, when the thought occurs to him that he may be losing his mind. Ultimately, it turns out, thoughts and memories are the cause of much emotional distress, particularly the kind that counseling can hope to alleviate or prevent. The pain of a physical wound produces emotional distress, but often not much can be done about that. The thought that one is disliked, or guilty, or selfish can also produce emotional distress. Perhaps something can be done about that.

It is with this view of man as a perceiving, thinking, feeling, reflective being that we now approach the causes of emotional distress. The nature of these causes of emotional distress is (1) sometimes circumstantial, (2) sometimes interpersonal, (3) sometimes physical, (4) sometimes conscious, (5) sometimes "unconscious," and (6) sometimes religious. We will take up each possibility in turn.

Circumstantial Causes of Distress

Frequently the unalterable circumstances of life cause people distress. For instance, the death of a family member or friend brings sorrow and grief. The loss of economic security brings anxiety and fear. Many people still living remember the Great Depression of the thirties with enough clarity to dread another. Automation and plant relocations have left people jobless and uncertain. Acts of nature like storms, tornados, and lightning bring their share of heartache.

Part of the distress arising from unavoidable circumstances comes, however, from how the person sees himself in relation to the situation. If he views the situation as beyond his control, he will probably be less disturbed by it than if he blames himself. But some people blame themselves for circumstances in their lives that are clearly beyond their control—for example, economic conditions that lead to job loss or business failure. This may represent unnecessary suffering. For people in all these and similar conditions the church has a ministry of comfort. The Gospel has within it a view of life that, if taken seriously, enables one to cope with the inevitable blows life deals. In many cases pastoral counseling is needed to help the individual see the relation of the Gospel to his life.

Interpersonal Causes of Distress

The behavior of other people frequently causes a person distress because of the complex interplays of emotional reactions that go on between people. Distress caused by the behavior of other people may be either intentional or inadvertent. On the one hand, people say and do things because they *want* to cause pain; they want to retaliate for some real or imagined wrong done to them. Sometimes people strike out at others when they are frustrated, angry, hurt, or threatened. Often the victim is the person who happens to be nearest or who can't strike back. On the other hand, people say and do things that cause distress without meaning to do so or without realizing that they are causing distress. Who has not unintentionally hurt someone's feelings? Who has not said or done the wrong thing at the wrong time? However, some of the inadvertent hurt that people do to one another results from deeply hidden motives of which they themselves are unaware. This is what psychiatrists and psychologists call "unconsciously" motivated behavior, a possibility discussed later in this chapter. Certainly, whatever the basis of the behavior, human beings cause each other an enormous amount of pain and misery. Much pastoral care is devoted to helping people cope with the distress caused by others—the thoughtless word, the intentional barb, the wayward son who grieves his parents, the unfaithful husband, the alcoholic wife.

Physical Causes of Distress

Almost all diseases and injuries give rise to some form of emotional distress. The most frequent type of initial distress is, of course, pain. Even a pinprick hurts. But pain is perceived, and it is thought about, remembered, and thought about again. This gives rise to another type of emotional distress—*fear*. The person who gets sick or is injured frequently has fears—fear of what the pain or injury may mean, fear of more injury or pain, fear of death. Still other reactions to illness are *anxiety* and *depression*. Even a slight skin rash can set some people worrying. For others the thought of impending dentistry or a visit to the doctor's office can create intense emotional distress.

Some kinds of physical illness produce so much emotional distress they stand out, and physicians recognize these as situations demanding special attention. Primary examples are tuberculosis, heart disease, cancer, and major surgery. To take only one, the dominant emotional reaction of tuberculosis patients involves fear and anxiety over a long period of time. Even when they have recovered physically to the extent possible, tuberculosis patients fear to return to normal life. They worry about relapse, about how they will be received by their friends, about obtaining jobs. Similarly, the strong emotional reactions that accompany heart conditions, cancer, and impending surgery are all familiar to the pastor. They constitute a major concern in his pastoral ministry.

A second type of distress phenomenon arises from disease and injury in the central nervous system, especially in the brain. These are known technically as *organic* mental disorders.[1] They include the following: mental disorder due to poisoning produced by chemicals, gases, and drugs; disorders resulting from infections that attack the nervous system; deterioration which accompanies old age; and abnormal conditions produced by injuries, brain tumors, and brain defects. Persons so impaired show a wide variety of symptoms, ranging all the way from loss of intellectual functions like memory and reasoning to emotional changes like anxiety, irritability, depression, and false euphoria. Whether or not the individual will recognize his own distress or admit that something is wrong varies among individuals. The diagnosis and treatment of these kinds of disorders belong almost exclusively to the medical profession. Nevertheless, the pastor has an obligation to minister even here, not as a physician or psychiatrist but as a minister of the Gospel.

Conscious Causes of Distress

The conscious psychological causes of emotional distress stem primarily from the way in which the person perceives himself, his circumstance, and other people. To put it into psychological jargon, this kind of emotional distress results from the person's "self-concept" and his "person-thing perceptions." This means that people constantly reflect on their status as persons. Many, if not most, engage in perpetual self-scrutiny, the basic questions of which are (1) "Am I all right as a person?" and (2) "How do other people see me?"

Thus the thoughts a person has about *himself* can be particularly painful. He asks himself such questions as: Am I a likeable person? Am I competent? Is my nose too prominent? Can I play basketball well enough to make the team? Is my family respected by others? Am I normal? He tells himself such things as: I'm losing my hair; I must look funny. I disappointed my parents; therefore I must be ungrateful. I masturbate; therefore I must be a sexual deviate. My mind wanders; something must be wrong with me. I think dirty and vulgar thoughts; I must be mentally ill. I feel frightened, and I don't know why; I may be losing my mind.

In a similar way, what a person thinks *other* people think

of him can be equally painful. He may ask: Are they laughing at me? Is my tie too loud? What must they think of me? What would the pastor say? He may tell himself: They *are* laughing at me. I'm so ashamed I can't bear to face them. If we buy a new car, people will think we've got money.

So it goes. People flagellate themselves with endless self-judgments and guesses about what others think of them. Out of all this mental activity comes an enormous amount of distress. The great bulk of it is mild but chronic. Few people recognize how much time they spend in such self-examining thought, and they are unaware of the extent to which other people worry about the same things. They are even less aware of how needless it all is.

The statement that much of this distress is needless raises the question of whether the distress is real. Sometimes one hears it said that such people merely imagine things. People accuse them of creating their own misery. They say this in a way that implies that if such people wanted to think and feel differently they could. Therefore, they imply, it's all their own fault. Therefore, they do not need sympathetic treatment or they are unworthy of it. Nothing could be farther from the truth. Such feelings, whether based on reality or not, are as real as anything under the sun. And controlling them is not a simple matter of what people call willpower. The psychological world of each person is *his* reality, regardless of what an outside observer thinks or sees. The pastor who wants to help such people cannot approach them with the idea that they are merely mistaken, silly, or self-indulgent. He can't even approach them with the hope of reasoning or arguing them out of their feelings. He must approach them sympathetically. More than that, if he wishes to help, he must try to understand their experiences not as *he* sees them but as *they* see them.

But how do people get that way? How do they get to be

such worrisome creatures? Partly it grows out of the American culture. From early childhood we Americans are taught to be concerned about whether we are all right and what others are thinking. Even infants become the object of such concerns. Parents worry, and say out loud that they worry, whether or not their children are as quiet as they ought to be, toilet-trained as early as they should be, as bright as they could be. Later, parents talk about what relatives and neighbors will think. They compare their children and even themselves to their friends. In addition, a good proportion of American advertising takes the form of the question "Are you all right?" Magazines, radio, and TV bombard us with questions that have within them a subtle threat. They ask: Do you have bad breath or body odor? Do you wear the latest fashions? Are you popular? Can you get and hold a man? Will you be the first kid in your block to own a widget? Do you smoke the right cigarettes and drink prestige liquor? Bust big enough or hips too big, madame? The whole culture is oriented toward critical self-examination. Everyone is encouraged to enter the rat race of social competition, and the insidious threat that one may not measure up looms everywhere. The result? Distress!

"Unconscious" Causes of Distress

The distress that comes from overly critical self-examination reflects only one side of the coin of psychologically caused distress, the side where the disturbing questions are in awareness and where the person knows, at least to a degree, the cause of his distress. But the coin has two sides. The other side reflects psychological distress caused by *unconscious* conflicts. Here the person cannot recognize the cause of his distress or sometimes even the fact that he is distressed. This takes us into the whole business of unconscious wishes, memories, impulses, and images.

The concept of unconscious mental processes came to prominence in psychology and psychiatry through the writings of Sigmund Freud.[2] Basically the notion is that parts of man's mental life are inaccessible to awareness under normal conditions. In Freudian theory personality consists of three parts: (1) the ego, or conscious part of self; (2) the superego, an unconscious, moral, judging part; and (3) the id, a base, sensuous, self-gratifying part, also unconscious. The unconscious parts of man lead a kind of independent mental existence. They think, they perceive, they remember, and they motivate man to action. Man is endowed with two basic drives, which bring about all behavior: the sexual drive, and an aggressive drive. Human behavior is always directed toward self-serving *sexual* or *aggressive* ends. But these drives and the thoughts, wishes, and memories connected with them are too threatening and painful to be recognized. The conscious part of self, the ego, cannot bear to face the true nature of the unconscious, especially the id. Therefore, these motives and the mental elements connected with them are kept out of awareness by an automatic censoring action, that is, they are *repressed*.

Much debate has gone on in psychology and psychiatry about the validity of the concept of unconscious motivation. Some, the followers of Freud naturally, take it very seriously, but others reject it. Psychologists have tried to demonstrate it empirically. At best they have only partly succeeded in presenting credible scientific evidence. Some therefore reject the concept on the grounds it can't be adequately demonstrated scientifically. Another group maintains that the concept *unconscious* refers to something genuine but that the Freudian description of it is too fanciful and unscientific because it implies an entity with an independent existence and "person-like" characteristics.

In the author's opinion, the word *unconscious* refers to

a real phenomenon, an important one for people who are concerned with emotional problems. In some ways it may be better to refer to it only as an *absence of awareness*. Thereby one avoids an undesirable type of speculation about the nature of "*the* unconscious" without denying the phenomenon. But however one labels it, the fact remains that people do seem to act on the basis of reasons of which they are not aware. Just as important, they seem to remember, perceive, and think unconsciously. Speculation about the nature of the phenomenon suggests that the whole process goes on as a series of neurological events in the brain. These neurological events somehow differ slightly from the ones that give rise to conscious thoughts. They are neurologically different in such a way that they do not become symbolized in the words and images of awareness. These neurological events permit the brain to function at a level outside of awareness.

The real issue here, however, is how memory, thinking, and motivation that go on without awareness can cause distress. The answer lies in the fact that they do not remain entirely outside of awareness. The neurological processes take place in such a way that fractional portions of unconscious memories, perceptions, and impulses do get into awareness. When they do, they disturb the individual. The person remembers, for example, an embarrassing incident from the past, or he recognizes a hostile or sexual urge in himself with shame and guilt. In addition, the *behavior* produced by unconscious motivation produces distress. For example, the person can't control his drinking, or he antagonizes other people without knowing how or why, or he feels sad and hopeless without apparent cause.

The question arises, however, why these distressing memories, perceptions, and impulses are blotted from awareness in the first place. The answer lies in past experiences, particularly childhood experiences. Such thoughts and impulses caused the individual pain and anxiety in the past. Sometimes they were punished, as when a child is spanked for hitting someone in anger. Sometimes they were intensely disapproved, as when a parent said, "If you do that again, you are not my little girl!" Sometimes they were threatened, as when a Sunday school teacher said, "God doesn't love little boys who steal." Even the memory of such things can cause pain. A merciful neurological event therefore intervenes to keep these memories, perceptions, impulses, and desires out of awareness. This is the phenomenon Freud called *repression.*

When repressed memories, perceptions, and impulses slip into awareness because of imperfect functioning of the neurological defense system, conscious distress results. Or they may find expression in behavior of which the person has no real understanding. Or they may be expressed as physical ailments like ulcers and hypertension (psychosomatic illness). These behavior patterns and physical illnesses reflect the underlying unconscious conflict between impulse and prohibition. They also constitute the symptoms of mental distress and sometimes of mental disorder. In the most penetrating forms of psychiatric treatment the goal is to make these unconscious memories, perceptions, and motives conscious so that they can be accepted by the person and handled more effectively.

Unconscious conflicts can, of course, reflect greater and lesser degrees of seriousness. Psychologists and psychiatrists maintain that everyone participates to some extent in the phenomenon. The difference between "normal" distress from unconscious processes and "mental disorder" is a matter of degree, not of kind. The pastor, of course, meets people with various degrees and kinds of distress. Part of his job as a competent, professional person is to take seriously the possibility that some of a person's distress may be unconscious in origin.

The above constitutes at best an incomplete description and rationale for what psychologists and psychiatrists call unconscious behavior. Perhaps some examples of this kind of behavior and the distress it produces will help.

The first example comes from a marital problem. A woman with a relatively passive husband constantly berated him for his lack of success in life. She pointed out other men who made more money, who got more frequent promotions, who, she said, "know what they want in life and go after it." At these times she was unhappy, dissatisfied, and jealous, and of course she made her husband miserable too. Not an unintelligent woman by any means, she wondered at times: "What gets into me?" She knew her husband was basically a good provider, kind, considerate, devoted. Therapy revealed that her shrewish behavior actually resulted from the fact that her husband was not as aggressive sexually as she would have liked. She had long entertained phantasies of being the wife of a bold, romantic lover, but modesty would not let her become sexually aggressive herself or tell her husband of her wishes. Without awareness (unconsciously), her criticisms really amounted to veiled complaints about her husband's lack of ardor and aggressiveness, and they contributed to their marriage problem.

An adolescent boy wanted desperately to have dates and go steady like others his age. He was reasonably good-looking, of average athletic ability, capable of carrying on an intelligent conversation, and yet he frequently found himself turned down on date invitations. When he did date a girl, it seldom went beyond one or two dates. Unhappy and depressed because he thought he was disliked by girls, he did not know that he was unusually self-defeating. It worked this way. Most of the girls he asked for dates were already going steady, and they were the most sought-after girls in town. So of course he received more than an average number of refusals. When a girl did accept his invitations, he worried that she did not like him. Then he dropped her before she had a chance to drop him. His past was strewn with mystified girls who could not understand why he never asked for another date. Far beneath all this surface behavior, the young man had a deep sense of social inadequacy because he did not really feel capable of attracting and holding a girl. Part of the problem dated back to the time in freshman high school when a girl told him she wouldn't go out with him if he was the last boy on earth. He was deeply hurt, but that had been forgotten (repressed), and he did not realize its impact on his later feelings and behavior.

Religious Causes of Distress

People also suffer distress that arises from religious concerns. Although the "death of God" theologian may feel that not many people worry about God or hell, there is probably more concern of this sort than is usually imagined. Judging from the responses received by evangelistic radio and television programs, a substantial group of people exist who grope constantly for satisfying religious answers. Many of them report unhappiness and dissatisfaction with their lack of religious commitment. Sometimes this has its origin in the guilt produced by early childhood religious training that they have neglected. Sometimes it comes from people with little or no religious training who have come to a realization of a burning need for religious answers to disturbing questions about life.

Religion can produce distress in another way. Church members may suffer from distress in the form of guilt feelings caused by religion but unrelieved by it. Some of this arises because the individuals engage in behavior their religious training condemns, and they feel guilty as a result. Some comes from the fact that people feel they should believe what the church teaches, and yet they know within themselves that they do not believe it. Some distress comes from doubts about whether their belief is strong enough. Evidence has accumulated that many people, adolescents particularly, have a much keener sense of guilt and religious inadequacy than they have of forgiveness and mercy.[3] If these findings are true, and there is little doubt that they are, it means that the essence of the Christian message of forgiveness has not been getting through properly. Clearly, a large area of pastoral responsibility remains to be worked out here.

Causes Viewed Theologically

If most people experience emotional distress some of the time, and if some people experience distress most of the time, we need to put this state of affairs into theological perspective. Christianity, which presumes to be related to the whole of life, must address itself to this situation. And this it does. The history of pastoral care is largely the history of how Christians have tried to make the Gospel relevant to people in distress.

Only the blindest optimist can look around the world today and not be impressed with the mess in which man finds himself. Wars and prospects of war fill the headlines. Disease and poverty are everywhere, while a small portion of the globe's population lives in affluence and luxury. Crime and corruption infest our cities. Families are torn by divorce and by children in open revolt against their parents. And this does not do justice to the total picture. In the face of this, one confronts two possible views of the nature of man. Both have a long history, and both can be found in the churches today.

One view tends to play down the severity of man's moral corruption and his responsibility for it. This view pictures man as basically good but somehow off the track. Due to some unfortunate (and unexplained) accident, man has gotten fouled up. But this view is at bottom optimistic about man, because it holds to the idea of his innate goodness. It asserts that man's goodness will ultimately triumph, and with the help of God he will eventually overcome his problems. An improved social order lies somewhere in the future. In some views man is seen as moving toward this better state as part of the process of evolution.

The other view is much more pessimistic about man. It sees man as deeply corrupted and contaminated. It does not flinch at the concept of sin, and it is willing to say that man's problems stem from his sinful nature. This quality of sin pervades man's whole being, and it contaminates everything he touches and does. Indeed, the whole of nature groans under this burden of sin. In short, man is evil, and he needs more than mere improvement. He needs a total redemption. This redemption is found in the Christ of the Gospel.

This second view of man best fits the panorama of distress we have pictured. As we have seen, distress pervades every aspect of man, physical and psychological, conscious and unconscious. Viewed theologically, this distress is one of the products of man's sinful nature. This includes distress of every sort — pain from injury and disease, fear and anxiety, shame and guilt, depression and loneliness, worry about one's relation to God, grief and sorrow — and every combination of these and other distressing experiences.

Christ the Cure

The Christian faith is that Christ redeems man from sin. When the Holy Spirit, working through Gospel and sacraments, gives a man personal faith in Christ as Savior, that person begins a new life. This new life involves a new attitude toward God, toward other people, and toward self. But it is only begun in the present. It is completed in the life to come. There all pain, sorrow, and distress are finally banished from human experience. In the meantime, in this present life, a person is a strange mixture of the new life in Christ and the old life contaminated by sin and its effects. Consequently human distress continues. It is this fact that makes pastoral care and counseling necessary. People need help with the distress of life. The pastor is in a unique position to help them.

The Pastor's Role

The average pastor cannot be a specialist on mental disorder, like the psychiatrist and psychologist. He can, however, become acquainted with the concepts and terminology of psychiatry and abnormal psychology. This we expect of all professional people who deal with human affairs— doctors, lawyers, educators. Furthermore, the pastor can be a specialist about *emotional distress.* We can expect him to be sensitive to the signs of emotional distress in people, and we can expect him to respond to them appropriately. The pastor is in a strategic position to help people cope with "normal" distress, because he is called on to help people bear the distress of life's burdens and crises. He can also help resolve the chronic but moderate distress of people who do not need psychiatric or psychological treatment. These two areas of pastoral service fall well within the limits of his professional responsibility.

> Man that is born of a
> woman is of few days,
> and full of trouble.
> —*Job 14:1*

2

Approaches from the Mental Health Professions

Emotional distress blends into the problem of mental disorder. It will help our cause in developing a point of view for pastoral counseling if we make a quick tour of the mental health field. Such a tour will provide some general information about this important and rapidly expanding field and some specific ideas that can later serve as reference points. The tour covers the professional groups involved, the types of treatment used for mental disorder, and certain ideas from psychoanalysis and client-centered therapy that are germane to our endeavor.

The Mental Health Professions

Professional Levels

We can order the professions concerned with problems of emotional distress and mental disorder into three categories in terms of the amount of training they have had and the proportion of their work devoted to emotional problems.

One group might be called the *"full-time* mental health professions." This group includes psychiatrists, clinical psychologists, and psychiatric social workers. Each is a specialty within a larger profession — psychiatry within medicine, clinical psychology within psychology, and psychiatric social work within social work. Members of these professions have 33 all had extensive specialized training for dealing with emotional disorder. They spend the bulk of their professional activity in treating people, in basic research, in administration of mental health facilities, or in training other professional people.

A second group of professional people deals with mental and emotional problems also, but only as a part of a larger sphere of professional activity. Their profession frequently brings them into contact with troubled people. This group includes physicians (other than psychiatrists), many psychologists, many educators, and some lawyers and judges. Clergymen are also in this group. People in these professions do not hold themselves out *primarily* as helpers of the distressed, yet they are likely to spend a significant amount of time counseling in one sense of that term or another. For example, the physician finds that many of his patients have personal problems that complicate their illness. The educator is approached by troubled students. Generally the amount of specific training members of these groups have for such work is small compared with that of the full-time mental health workers. This limits sharply their capacity to help, and they rely heavily on referral to the full-time professions and to mental health facilities when they encounter problems beyond their competence.

A third group of people, not professional, also plays a major part in dealing with distress. This is the group that for lack of a better term might be called "other people." Parents, relatives, friends, neighbors, police, scout leaders, and kindly gray-haired old grandfathers all have a stake in this. No one knows for certain how much good or how much harm they do. Probably when the distress is not severe and the underlying problems not critical, they are very helpful. When severe problems arise or when the problem involves actual mental disorder, the possibility exists that they can do harm.

Treatment

Basic approaches for the treatment of mental disorder used by the mental health professions are (1) physical treatment methods, (2) psychotherapy and counseling in which the person talks about himself and his problems, and (3) conditioning methods in which the systematic application of reinforcement and nonreinforcement (rewards and punishments) is used to shape behavior. Behavior conditioning methods are quite recent developments based on some long-established principles of conditioning, but they involve highly technical issues that are beyond the scope of this book.

Physical Treatment Methods

Physical treatment methods work directly on the human body. They manipulate a body part, change body chemistry, alter physical functioning. As such they fall strictly within the practice of medicine. Three main varieties of physical treatment are used with mental disorder: drug therapy, shock therapy, and psychosurgery. Of these three, drug therapy is employed by the entire medical profession, but shock therapy and psychosurgery are practiced only by suitably trained physicians.

The use of drugs having narcotic and pain-killing properties with emotionally distressed patients has a history as long as medicine itself. A significant advance in the use of drugs for psychiatric treatment occurred in about 1955, however, when several new types of drugs became available. These drugs have remarkable effects on mentally disturbed people. A major difference between the effect of these new drugs and the older drugs is that they produce relief from emotional symptoms and distress without producing heavy sedation in the patient. The patient experiences relief without becoming excessively sleepy, slowed down physically, or insensitive to his surroundings. Frequently the patient can go about his usual activities while taking the drug under a physician's supervision. These drugs can be put into three main classes: simple tranquilizers, antipsychotic tranquilizers, and anti-depressants.

Simple tranquilizers (sometimes called the minor tranquilizers) are widely prescribed by physicians for the relief of tension and anxiety. Their use is not restricted to people with acute mental disorder. Trade names like Miltown and Equanil have become household words. The simple tranquilizers reduce "normal" stress and tension, and they are especially suitable for cases of neurotic anxiety, psychosomatic illness, insomnia, tension headaches, and menstrual difficulties. They have little in the way of undesirable side effects when taken under a physician's care.

The antipsychotic tranquilizers (sometimes called major tranquilizers) have much more dramatic effects than the simple tranquilizers. In addition to their calming effect, they reduce symptoms of severe mental disorder like hallucinations, delusions, withdrawn behavior, stupor, extreme agitation. They are used in heavy dosage in mental hospitals where the patient can be watched carefully for adverse side effects. Dosage for the nonhospitalized patient is normally less, but close supervision by a physician is still necessary.

The antidepressant drugs (sometimes called psychic energizers) are the latest addition to the armamentarium of psychiatric drugs. They are particularly useful in the treatment of severe depression. They work by acting on the central nervous system as a stimulant or depressant or both. Sometimes they are used with one of the major tranquilizers to give a kind of two-pronged attack: antipsychotic and antidepressant.

Drug therapies do not cure mental distress and disorder in the usual sense of the word *cure*. That is, they do not remove the cause of the difficulty; they provide symptom removal. If the drug is removed, the patient usually suffers a relapse unless his emotional problems have been altered while drug therapy was being used. Needed for a cure is a change in the person's manner of coping with himself and his life circumstances. The latter is, of course, the goal of counseling and psychotherapy. Nevertheless, recent developments in drug therapy constitute a major breakthrough in the treatment of mental disorders and distress. The future of this field lies wide open and looks very promising.

Once widely used but now diminishing in use, *shock therapy* was the first significant development in the treatment of mental illness by a specific physical method. The basic medical procedure is to produce a coma in the patient by creating a condition of partial anoxia (lack of oxygen) in the brain by using insulin or electric shock. When the brain is deprived of oxygen to the point where normal cerebral function cannot be supported, the person goes into a coma. This is accompanied by other physical reactions typical of a state of shock. For reasons that are largely unknown some patients show marked improvement after a series of such shock treatments. Shock therapy is falling into disuse because drug therapy does the same job so much more efficiently. One mental condition for which it continues to be used with some frequency, however, is severe depression, where it is reported to be as high as 90 percent effective. Strangely enough, the use of shock is continuing much longer in private practice than in mental hospitals. The reason for this is understandable. The psychiatrist often finds himself dealing with a patient who has a family to support or a household to manage, and he wants to get the person functioning again as soon as he can for very practical reasons. If other methods (drugs or psychotherapy) fail, he tries shock treatment in a local hospital, because he wants to avoid sending the person to a mental hospital if possible.

The last physical treatment method to be considered is psychosurgery or, more accurately, lobotomy. This method of treating acutely distressed mental patients has now been practically abandoned. Several types of operation were developed. The basic technique involved entering the skull cavity and severing some of the connections between the frontal lobes of the brain and the thalamus. In a general way the frontal lobes seem to govern self-reflection and anticipation of the future, and the thalamus appears to activate strong emotions. It was found that if some connections between this emotional center and the thought centers were severed, the patient sometimes lost his agitation and distress. Lobotomy was a radical treatment procedure involving irreversible destruction of brain tissue.

Psychotherapy and Counseling

Some workers make a distinction between *psychotherapy* and *counseling*. Psychotherapy then usually refers to talking treatment that aims to dig deeply into the person's personality structure to find the causes of mental disorder and to make major changes in the personality to improve the person's situation. Such a goal requires prolonged treatment, as much as four to six sessions a week for two or more years. If such a distinction is made, counseling then refers to treatment that attempts to help a person solve only one or a few specific problems: a marriage problem, a problem of vocational choice, a school adjustment problem. The counseling focuses on problem *solution* rather than major personality reorganization. The length of treatment may be fairly long (one or two sessions a week for several months) or rather short (a dozen sessions or less). In both types of treatment a trained therapist is needed.

The way the terms *counseling* and *psychotherapy* are used among mental health professionals is not always sharp and clear. To some extent the distinction depends on what the professional person chooses to call his activities. A psychiatrist or psychologist may refer to all his work involving discussion with another person as "psychotherapy." Some psychologists dislike the term *therapy* because of its medical implications and use only the term *counseling*. Social workers usually refer to their activities as *case work counseling*.

For our purposes, we have chosen three basic approaches for consideration: authority-oriented counseling, psychoanalysis, and client-centered therapy.

Authority-Oriented Counseling

Few professional mental health workers today do what we will describe as "authority-oriented counseling." To some extent what follows amounts to a caricature of the inept therapist or the counseling done by people who do what seems to them to be the logical thing to help another person. The description constitutes a kind of lesson in what good counseling is not, and we present it for that reason.

In this type of counseling, when a person comes to another person for help, he almost always looks upon the counselor as someone who knows the answers and can give solutions. The authority-oriented counseling approach plays on this attitude, and the counselor takes on the air of a specialist. In words and manner he says to the troubled person: "Tell me your problem, and I will tell you what to do about it." He proceeds to ask questions, give advice, and provide assurance that everything will turn out all right if the person will just do as he is told.

Several fatal assumptions underlie this kind of approach: First, there is the assumption that the counselor is an expert who can, in a short time, diagnose the cause of the person's difficulty. Trained therapists generally agree that counseling and psychotherapy constitute a mutual endeavor in which both the person and the counselor have an expert role to play.

The person is the "expert" in reporting how he experiences himself and his situation. The counselor is the expert in helping him explore himself more deeply and completely and perhaps find the meaning of these experiences. Authority-oriented counseling tends to impede the exploration process by creating a gulf in which the counselor is seen as superior and the person as inferior. This gulf often makes the person afraid to explore his true inner feelings, especially those that are embarrassing or painful. It also makes the person overly dependent on the counselor, which in some cases is the very problem the person needs to solve.

Second, authority-oriented counseling assumes that the sources of the person's difficulties are easy to find and conscious in nature. The authority-oriented counselor may take but a few minutes, or at best a few hours, to hear the person's problem. Then the counselor stands ready to give advice. In problems of any magnitude this is simply not adequate. Experience suggests that it often takes months for a person to find within himself the causes of his difficulties. Authority-oriented counseling, by contrast, is prone to deal in clichés and superficial causes, take naïvely everything the person says at its face value, and base its solutions on an inadequate knowledge of the problem.

Third, authority-oriented counseling proceeds on the assumption that there are neat, specific remedies for the person's difficulty. If the person becomes tense in social situations, he is told to go to social affairs or to join a church and meet people until he overcomes his discomfort. If he has trouble with school grades, he is told to make out a daily study schedule. If he is anxious, he is told to stop worrying and think along more constructive lines.

Finally, authority-oriented counseling assumes that the person can use the advice supplied by the counselor by simply making up his mind to do so. If the person could take up and use such homilies, he might be helped. But he has usually received exactly the same advice previously from well-meaning authorities or friends. In fact, if it were that easy, he would have been over the problem long ago, and he would never have come to the counselor in the first place.

Although we have caricatured authority-oriented counseling, we readily acknowledge that it is by no means completely ineffectual and worthless. We have no way to estimate the amount of help given by nonprofessional people to each other in the form of advice, comfort, sympathy, encouragement. But the pastor should be aware of the fallacies and shortcomings of this approach. It is the method he is most likely to find himself inclined to use. The pastor needs to develop a healthy skepticism about quick analysis of problems and easy advice-giving. He should know why professional psychotherapists are more than a little critical. The fact is that such methods may be valuable in inverse relation to the severity of a problem. That is, they may work best with simple problems of everyday living. (Or perhaps they do not do much harm, and the person eventually solves the problem himself.) They work least well in more serious problems. If the pastor wishes to think of himself as one who can help persons with more serious kinds of distress, it is incumbent on him to have a more effective counseling approach than authority-oriented counseling.

Psychoanalysis

Psychoanalysis began its ascent as a major school of thought in psychiatry just before the turn of the century. Psychoanalysis is both a theory of how personality develops and a method of treatment for mental disorder. It is too elaborate and complex for detailed description here. We focus on how, according to this theory, the need for treatment arises, some of the procedures used in therapy, and some of the phenomena that occur during treatment that the pastor may encounter in his own counseling.

How do people get into difficulty psychologically? Based on extensive experience with treatment of mental disorder, psychoanalysis asserts that all people start life with two sets of basic motivational impulses—sex and aggression. Sexual motivation is broadly conceived and includes all sources of sensual gratification through mouth, anus, genital apparatus, eyes, ears, and skin. Aggression is also broadly conceived and covers all forms of self-assertion. It is particularly characterized, however, by hostile and destructive impulses, and these can be directed either outward to others or upon one's self. While these two motivational thrusts find their basic origin in biological energy, they manifest themselves primarily in the form of *psychic* (psychological) energy. Psychic energy in turn controls behavior, including the kind found in emotional distress.

We can picture it this way. The child starts out life with a normal complement of psychic energy pressing for expression. At first the infant seeks gratification of his sexual and aggressive impulses without regard for anyone else and without concern about the means used in seeking the gratification. While parents are indulgent with the newborn infant, picking it up when it cries, feeding it when it is hungry, changing it when it is wet or soiled, this blissful state of affairs does not last long. Beginning about the time he starts to walk, the child encounters something other than unlimited tender loving care. The parents want him to start to shape up to their idea of what a child should be like. They begin to approve and disapprove, and they show their disapproval through anger, threats, and displeasure when the child does not meet their hopes and expectations. Eating, toilet training, displays of self-assertion, anger, and sexual interests become focal points of parental approval and disapproval.

At first, lacking language, the child can only sense disapproval emotionally, but later he comes to understand both the spoken and unspoken disapproval and threats of the parents. He is caught. By nature he has strong impulses to gratify in the most direct way possible. At the same time, the disapproval and punishment of the parents are a potent counterforce. The parents want him to eat nicely and on schedule, to learn bowel and bladder control, to stop hitting other children and throwing blocks in a tantrum. They are alarmed at his interest in sex and his childish sexual activity. The child senses their disapproval as a severe threat to his well-being. His immature mind sees them threatening to withdraw their love and support, perhaps even to abandon or kill him.

He has only one choice. He must control the disapproved impulses. These impulses must somehow be bound so that they cannot produce unacceptable behavior. When they do produce unacceptable behavior, or even when they only threaten to do so, they produce intolerable *anxiety,* an acute type of distress. But *repression* comes to the child's aid. Repression controls the anxiety by driving the unacceptable impulses and the memory of them out of consciousness. Under favorable conditions, where parents are understanding and not too threatening, only the most socially unacceptable impulses have to be repressed, and a reasonably normal person results. Under pathological conditions, however, the threat to withdraw love and support from the child accompanies many or most of the child's expressions of aggression, self-assertion, and sexuality. The parents, and later other adults, punish and disapprove too broad a spectrum of these activities. Then the child has no choice but to repress large areas of behavior. Almost all sex and aggression become dangerous. Deprived of an adequate means of expression, these impulses erupt first in frightening dreams and anxiety, and finally in the symptoms of mental disorder.

Distress and the symptoms of mental disorder always express in some devious way the underlying conflict between forbidden impulses and their control. For example, the high blood pressure of hypertension may reflect repressed anger. The loss of vision of the hysterically blind person may reflect escape from some threatening sight of the past. The delusions of the psychotic may represent a vain attempt to ward off overwhelming anxiety by reconstructing the world in a new, nonthreatening, but bizarre way. Common distress like worry, unhappiness, and lack of self-confidence can be milder expressions of similar conflicts in less seriously disturbed persons. This is known as "the language of symptoms," and it forms a fascinating subject. The goal of psychoanalytic treatment is to have the person explore his early experiences and relearn how to live with his own nature. This means strengthening the repression of some impulses but relaxing and allowing the expression of others.

We turn next to look at the psychoanalytic treatment approach. In *classical* psychoanalysis, the patient is seen from four to six times a week for a 50-minute hour. He reclines on a couch as comfortably as he can. The analyst sits at the head of the couch in such a position that he can observe the patient but the patient cannot see the analyst without craning his neck. Especially during the early months of treatment the analyst has relatively little to say. The purpose of this arrangement is to keep the analyst as impersonal as possible. Thus any feelings and attitudes the patient develops toward the analyst are largely projections from the patient rather than reactions to the analyst's actual personality. The analyst lays upon the patient what Freudians call the *fundamental rule*. The fundamental rule is that during the treatment hour the patient must tell everything that comes into his mind. This is not the easiest thing to do. Analysands have a marked tendency to hold back thoughts during the analytic hour because they are too painful or embarrassing, because they appear too trivial, because the mind seems to go blank.

Closely related to the fundamental rule is the process known as *free association.* The patient is expected to put his mind in neutral gear and let the ideas, images, feelings, and memories flow freely. He is expected to report any dreams he has and to free-associate to them. It takes several weeks in treatment to learn to free-associate adequately. The goal of the free-associative activity is to lead the patient and the analyst back into the person's childhood to recapture the thoughts, images, experiences, feelings, and memories that were involved in the development of his emotional difficulties. In this way the patient relives the causes of his problems and, it is to be hoped, learns to sort out the distortions and inappropriate reactions and find better ways of feeling and living.

Variations of the psychoanalytic method have been developed. Some of the same basic procedures are used with patients who are seen only once or twice a week or in group therapy. Child analysis is carried out in special play-therapy rooms, where the child is allowed to reveal his conflicts through play.

When this kind of treatment procedure is employed by a trained psychoanalyst (a specialist within psychiatry who has several years training beyond a psychiatric residency), several phenomena emerge. They also appear in other forms of counseling and psychotherapy, including pastoral counseling, so they are worthy of our attention.

One phenomenon is called *resistance.* This is the tendency every patient has to avoid revealing himself because of the anxiety this creates. Resistance shows itself by violations of the fundamental rule, in blocking, missing appointments, and other forms of lack of cooperation. Some of this may be deliberate and conscious, but more often it is not. Even though the person wants to do what is expected, he fails to do so. His own defenses keep him from talking freely and remembering vital material.

Another phenomenon in analysis is called *transference.* Transference refers to irrational feelings the patient develops toward the therapist. These may be fears that the therapist is going to reject the patient—for example, fear that the therapist will say the patient is incurable or too disgusting to be treated. Or the transference may show itself in a wish to have the therapist love him, or protect him like a child, or feed him, or seduce him. All these feelings come from the patient. They reflect fears, wishes, and impulses the patient had toward his parents and parent substitutes as a child. The transference becomes, for the analyst, the clue to how the patient became ill. Transference reactions betray the pathological relationships between the child and his family and friends that gave rise to his problems.

It is interesting to note that the therapist also develops transference feelings toward the patient. This is known as *countertransference,* and it is because of countertransference that the analyst himself is psychoanalyzed during his training. This enables him to recognize these feelings for what they are, derivatives of his own childhood experiences. In this way they can be kept from interfering with the treatment process.

When the initial resistances to treatment have been met and overcome and the transference has developed and the analyst has begun to see the nature of the problem and its origin, two additional activities take place. The therapist helps the patient to *work through* his feelings and memories. That is, the person goes over them again and again until they lose their anxiety-provoking ability and can be accepted into consciousness. For example, the patient may have to talk through on several occasions the fact that he engaged in perverse childhood sexual activities. At first it is painful and embarrassing to admit this, but as the patient works it through, the guilt diminishes and the patient can live easier with this aspect of his past.

The other activity the therapist undertakes is *interpretation.* The analyst explains to the patient how he came to feel and be the way he is. But this is not mere intellectual explanation, which is deemed useless. It is carefully timed and phrased so that the explanation produces an "aha!" response of emotional insight in the patient, and this requires skill. If the interpretation comes too soon, it will be wasted. If it comes too late, the precious moment of emotional insight will be lost. Gradually, over months and months, patient and analyst dig deeper and deeper into the patient's personality. If all goes well, the person discovers how he came to be the way he is, and his behavior patterns change. He loses his symptoms. He feels more comfortable with himself. He takes on more mature ways of acting.

We shall have occasion to refer to *resistance, transference, working through,* and *interpretation* in later chapters.

Client-Centered Therapy

Like psychoanalysis, the client-centered approach is largely the product of one man's initiative and insight and was born of his efforts to help people in distress. The man is a prominent American psychologist, Carl R. Rogers. The client-centered approach has gained widespread attention among educators and clergymen who are interested in counseling. Unlike psychoanalysis, which is a medical specialty within a specialty, the client-centered approach is aimed at everyone who hopes to help the distressed. As with psychoanalysis, we will look briefly at its conception of how man gets into difficulty and then at some of its ideas about therapy and counseling.[4]

Early in life, according to client-centered thinking, something important happens to an individual. He learns as a result of his experiences to value approval and positive regard from others and to be anxious about reactions from others that connote disapproval and criticism. This begins with the approving and disapproving reactions of parents, but eventually the individual begins to make the same kinds of "good—bad" evaluations about himself. These evaluations are incorporated into a picture or estimate of self called the *self-concept.*

The self-concept includes such diverse attitudes and self-perceptions as the *me* that plays piano poorly, the *me* that grew an inch last year, the *me* that won the prize in English composition, the *me* that thinks dirty thoughts, the *me* I would like to be, the *me* that hates housework, the *me* that is afraid of sickness and pain. The self-concept is fluid, that is, it changes with new experiences, but it tends to be reasonably stable over time in most people. While it is largely the product of slow experience by experience-learning, it can also be changed drastically by a single experience. A sharp criticism, an unexpected compliment, an important accomplishment or failure, or a series of such experiences can change a person's concept about a particular aspect of himself. For example, a middle-aged man lost his job, and he was unable to find employment. He soon developed a concept of himself as "an unemployable man over forty." It is out of such self-evaluations that much pain and distress are born.

Trends in self-appraisal are not necessarily all in a single direction, all positive or all derogatory. A person may feel he is acceptable in one respect and unacceptable in another, but there is usually an overall trend of self-rejection or self-acceptance. Just as important, the self-concept may contain distortions based on misperceptions, incorrect self-evaluations, and reactions from other people who are themselves distorted in their thinking. To a large degree, the measure of an individual's pathology is the number of aspects of himself that he is misjudging, for whatever reason. When a person's perceptions of himself are in line with the way things really are, he is "normal." When there is distortion, he is in difficulty and may need help.

Client-centered counselors avoid the use of terms like *mental illness* and *patient* because they believe the terms are inappropriate. For them, what some people call mental illness amounts to distortion between the way a person sees himself and other people (and the way he acts as a result) and the way things actually are. The goal of psychotherapy is to reduce this distortion or *incongruence*. Generally speaking, a person who needs therapy is a person who has many misperceptions of himself and the world of either a negative, self-depreciating nature or of a grandiose, self-flattering nature. Furthermore, the way a person sees himself and feels about himself determines much of, if not all, his behavior. The person who has a realistic, positive self-picture will be a happy, productive individual. The person who is caught in a web of self-depreciation and self-rejection or in false self-aggrandizement will reflect this both in emotional distress and in his actions.

Rogers and the client-centered group have developed very explicit ideas about what constitutes counseling. In the first place, for counseling to take place, two persons must be in *psychological contact*. This means that each of the two parties must experience the other to some extent. Normally this takes place through direct visual and auditory contact in a counseling interview.

Second, when he is doing counseling, the therapist must be *congruent* in the counseling relationship. That is, he must be undefensive, open about what is going on, open and honest about himself, not distorting reality. It is not necessary that he be this all the time outside of counseling. He does not have to be a superadjusted being, but when he is with a client he must not be playing roles—for example, the role of the great counselor who is all-wise or the role of the flawlessly adjusted human who will help the less fortunate. Therapists are tempted to play these and many other roles, all of which get in the way of therapy. He must also be open with himself about his own emotional problems. When the person touches on material that is problematic for the counselor—for example, something he himself fears, dislikes, or desires—he must be open enough to recognize this in himself.

Third, the therapist must have *unconditional positive regard* for the person he is trying to help. This means he accepts that person regardless of who or what he is, what he says or does, and what he wants or intends. In describing this characteristic of the therapist, words like *warm, accepting, concerned, nonmanipulative,* and *nonpossessive* best catch Rogers' meaning. It is recognized that a person cannot have one-hundred-percent unconditional positive regard for another person all the time, but it is expected that this attitude will characterize the counseling. Unconditional positive regard is the essential ingredient for an atmosphere conducive to healthy psychological change and growth.

Fourth, the therapist must experience *empathic* understanding of the client's perceptions of himself and his world. He should "feel" his way into the client's perceptions. To have empathic understanding is to "crawl inside another person's world," to understand in some depth how the other person feels and how he sees things, to sense what the other person is experiencing. The notion is not that the therapist is some omniscient being who can magically know everything a person feels, but rather that the therapist deliberately tries to be sensitive to what the person is expressing in words, facial expression, body position, and gestures. This requires him to be constantly alert to nuances in the client's words and actions that may convey his inner experience.

Finally, the therapist must somehow *communicate* to the client that he possesses the above characteristics. This means that the client has to experience the therapist's openness and nondefensiveness (congruence), the deep regard and respect the therapist has for him as a person, and the empathic understanding the therapist has of him. There are things the counselor does to convey these attitudes to the client. He does it first of all by what he *is*. If he is these things — open, honest, empathic — the client soon comes to sense this. He does it secondly by the way he responds during counseling to what the client says and does. This constitutes the "technique" of counseling. He shows his understanding and unconditional acceptance by responding to the feelings and perceptions of the client and *reflecting* them back to him. He shows the client he understands and accepts by putting the client's experience into words.

What can a person expect if he goes to a client-centered counselor? Will he be asked to lie on a couch? to free-associate? to report dreams? None of these is likely to happen. He will meet a person, perhaps for the first time in his life, who truly tries to understand him and seems to show it. He will receive no advice and no interpretations. He will not even be asked questions about his problems. It is contrary to client-centered practice to ask questions, to probe, to evaluate the person, to give advice or interpretations, or even to reassure, comfort, or console. The counselor directs his efforts to trying to understand what the client is experiencing during the counseling hour and what he has experienced outside of counseling.

When the counselor believes he has captured something of the client's experience, he puts it into words, *symbolizes* it for him. The actual statements of the counselor are few in number, and they are usually brief. The client is allowed to carry the conversation wherever he wishes. No particular premium is placed on the past, since it is believed that problems can often be resolved in terms of their present manifestations without a reconstruction of the experiences that led up to them. No particular emphasis is placed on uncovering hidden or "repressed" memories or motives, as in psychoanalysis. But the client is literally free to say anything he wishes. The counselor will not react with shock or judgmental statements. He will not try to persuade the client to accept a particular interpretation of his experiences or to adopt a particular course of action. He directs his efforts to helping the person experience himself more fully.

In contrast to psychoanalysis, client-centered counseling usually involves only one session a week, or perhaps two sessions. It may run from a few weeks to a year or more.

What do client-centered counseling clients talk about in therapy? Everything under the sun — their fears, their wishes, their past experiences, their feelings in the counseling hour, their sex life, their friends, their relatives, their successes, their failures, their loves, their hates — in short, everything that has ever bothered a human being is likely to come up. But this, of course, is what people talk about in counseling anywhere, assuming the therapist allows the person to do most of the talking and lets him talk about what bothers him.

Client-centered counselors find, however, fairly predictable trends in counseling. At first the person starts out with his problems and usually with a number of negative attitudes toward himself. In the early stages of counseling the number of expressed negative attitudes is likely to get even larger, but eventually the person begins to question his own feelings and reactions toward himself. He discovers aspects of himself that were previously unavailable to him. Then he begins to change his self-concept in a more positive direction. He is also likely to begin to feel that he has greater control over his own behavior than he had previously and to start acting differently. He is likely to end by working out a new set of values and feelings about himself and his world.

3

Approach for Pastors: Basic Considerations

A pastor needs some well-spelled-out ideas about what he does to help distressed people and why he does it. One gets the impression that pastors want to do *counseling* but that they have only vague ideas about what counseling really is and how to go about it. They seem insecure and prone to develop guilt feelings because of this lack of certainty. Such concern is quite understandable. In the last four or five decades psychiatry, clinical psychology, and social work have taken over responsibilities that were previously almost the exclusive domain of the minister, the family physician, and kindly old grandfathers. These newer professions have developed terminology, rationales, and techniques that seem superior to those of the pastor, leaving him in a position of uncertainty.

This book takes a specific viewpoint on the goals, certain key decisions, methods, and limits of competence of the pastor in counseling. No claim is made that this is the only possible approach. We present it as one that we hope will prove useful to the pastor. *Finally, however, the pastor must make his own decisions about the counseling enterprise.* He can best arrive at such decisions by widespread reading about counseling and psychotherapy, taking seminary and university courses when he has the opportunity, and attending lectures, conferences, and workshops. Nothing can substitute for broad study and experience, especially experience gained under supervision. For this reason, participation in clinical training programs is   *53* especially valuable. Ultimately, however, each pastor must work out his own philosophy and methods. The author believes that something close to the approach described here will best suit the ministerial profession. He believes equally strongly, indeed more strongly, that the only useful approach is one a person has arrived at by his own study and experience.

We examine next three basic considerations for pastoral counseling. They can be put in the form of questions: (1) What are the pastor's goals in working with distressed persons? (2) Will the pastor offer the distressed person pastoral care or counseling? (3) How permissive or directive will he be?

The Goals of Counseling

By far the most important issue in pastoral counseling is the matter of objectives. It is critical for the pastor to know what he is trying to accomplish. It is not enough for him to say he wants to *help people*. Neither good intentions nor such a vague objective is adequate to undergird counseling. The pastor needs to have specific and well-formulated (verbalizable) goals.

One way to approach the question of goals is to look first at the goals of professional mental health workers. What are their objectives as they ply their professional trade? The goals of secular counseling and psychotherapy are (1) to alleviate emotional distress by whatever means are available and (2) to help the person fulfill his potential as a human being. Much is summed up in those two objectives, of course. They imply such goals as resolving conflicts, reducing anxiety, removing symptoms, helping the person hold a job, and helping the person become a responsible citizen. But the main objectives are to alleviate distress and to help the person realize his potential.

We assume that the pastor shares in these objectives in his own approach to counseling. In fact, we assume that these

objectives enter to some extent into all his ministerial functions — visiting the sick, working with youth, preaching, teaching, and evangelism. He too wants to alleviate distress and
to help people become all that their potential will permit.

The critical question is, In what way are the pastor's
objectives different? What does he seek to do that the secular
helping professions do not do? What makes his work as a
minister unique? In a sense, we thus ask what right the pastor
has to a place among the helping professions. For if the pastor
merely wants to "help people," plenty of other professional
people want to do that, and many of them are much better
prepared for the task than he is. They have a unique service
to offer as physician, lawyer, educator, psychologist, or social
worker. Unless he has a specific role to play in helping people,
the pastor has little claim to a place among the helping
professions.

The pastor's special sphere of service is in relation to the
individual's spiritual welfare. His concern is for the relationship of the individual to God and to his fellowman. And the
pastor's basic goal, we believe, is singular: *It is to put right
the relationship between man and God by conveying the Word
of God concerning Jesus Christ to man.* Broadly construed,
this includes both of the goals of the helping professions,
alleviating distress and helping the individual achieve his
full potential. But his concern for the spiritual dimension
lends these objectives a unique quality, and this unique
quality gives the pastor claim to a place among the helping
professions. Let's spell this out a bit.

Man's essential problem is his alienation from God, which
results from sin. Man's sinful nature and his sinful behavior
have separated him from God and worked havoc among men.
Ultimately sin is at the bottom of all man's physical and
mental distress. It is also what prevents him from reaching
his full potential as a human being. To alleviate distress at

its source, the breach with God must be healed. To free man to be all the Creator intended him to be, that is, to realize his full potential, the results of sin must be remedied. Man must be reunited with God again, and the gulf bridged. The pastor's unique function is to be about the business of mending this break by means of the Gospel of Jesus Christ.

Let us append two notes to the last statement immediately, however. One is that the alleviation of distress and the attainment of human potential remain incomplete in this present life. To be completely free from all sorrow, pain, and hurt and to be all that one's potential permits is a final state attained only in the kingdom of God that is coming. In the present, man is always in the process of *becoming.*

The other note is that healing the separation from God through the Gospel is not the only means of alleviating distress and helping people fulfill their potential. The minister only embarrasses himself when his claims are extravagant. The physician alleviates distress regularly by using only drugs, surgery, or even rest. The lawyer alleviates distress by righting a legal injustice, defending a client, settling a dispute. The educator helps people achieve their potential by replacing ignorance with knowledge, by equipping them to earn a living, and by helping them understand themselves and the world around them. The psychiatrist, psychologist, and social worker commonly alleviate distress and help a person realize his potential by helping him understand his feelings, his strengths and weaknesses, and by helping him cope with life more effectively. The pastor's work is more basic. It gets at the root of the problem, because it resolves the essence of man's difficulty, his separation from God.

How does the pastor achieve his objectives? As already indicated, he does it by conveying the Word of God regarding Jesus Christ to people. Strictly speaking, the pastor does not do it at all. God does it, working through the Gospel as it is conveyed in the spoken, written, pictured Word and in the sacraments. The pastor is only a tool, a means of communicating the Gospel. He can easily stand in the way of God's Word by being the wrong sort of person. But it is not the pastor's power but God's power that accomplishes the task of making the Gospel effective in men's lives.

The message the pastor conveys has two elements. On the one hand, it confronts the individual with his sin. It shows him God's judgment upon mankind and upon himself because of sin. He stands defenseless before his Maker, stripped bare of any claim on God's mercy. God's law condemns him and all mankind. On the other hand, just as quickly as this message of condemnation is announced, just so quickly comes the Gospel – the gracious promise of God's love and forgiveness in Christ. The message that the pastor conveys says clearly that, although the individual is a sinner, God loves the sinner. God has acted in history to remedy the tragic state in which man finds himself because of his sinful nature. God has sent His Son, Jesus Christ, to redeem the world. The life, the death, the resurrection of Jesus Christ is man's salvation. Through Christ, God heals the breach and draws man back to himself. This Gospel – good news – is to all who believe and accept it the pledge of God's forgiveness.

In that comforting promise of God's love and acceptance can lie alleviation of the distress that sin produces *directly* – fear of God, guilt over sin, feelings of alienation, and a sense of meaninglessness to life. It may also alleviate the distress that sin produces *indirectly* – general anxiety, mental symptoms, even physical distress. In that Gospel also lies freedom – freedom to become all that one's potential permits. Having to fear neither God nor man, the individual can live courageously, boldly. Freed from guilt and from a sense of alienation or meaninglessness, man is in a position to live creatively and joyfully. A man's life gains direction because he knows that the purpose of life is to serve God and his fellowman. In this way both objectives of the helping professions are met when the pastor communicates the Word of God effectively.

If the pastor accepts the idea that his objective as a professional person is to communicate this two-pronged message, it will color his whole attitude and approach to pastoral care and counseling. He will not merely seek to get Mrs. Jones to worry less, or patch up the Schmidt marriage, or get Jim to quit drinking and bring home his paycheck. He will try to get these people to see their lives and their problems in the light of God's will and God's love for them. The goal of counseling becomes not just one of alleviating distress; it becomes one of alleviating distress by helping the person acknowledge his sin and alienation, accept God's forgiveness, and live the new life in Christ. How this is done in the preaching and teaching work of the minister is not hard to see. There he is constantly holding before his people God's judgment, His mercy in Christ, and the new life. How the pastor works this message into his counseling is another, very complex matter. In good counseling the counselor does not simply barge in with a message irrespective of the person's problem. Counseling is primarily a matter of the person exploring and experiencing himself, with the counselor acting as a facilitating agent. We will take up the issue of how and when the pastor brings in his basic message later under the concept of *confrontation*.

The pastor should make a major decision about his goal. He should decide whether or not he accepts the thesis that his major goal in counseling is ultimately to convey the Gospel to the individual. If his decision is negative on this question, the author would say that he has an inappropriate understanding of the nature of the ministry. His saying this is without rancor or heat, but it is firm and unequivocal. If his decision is in agreement on this point, this will have a decided effect on his efforts to relieve distress and help people achieve their potential.

Pastoral Counseling or Pastoral Care?

Once the pastor has made the decision about his objectives, another basic question arises: Is he going to provide pastoral *care?* Or is he going to offer pastoral *counseling?* The two obviously overlap, but there are also important differences between them.

With the development of the mental health professions, the word *counseling* has taken on a restrictive meaning. It can no longer be applied properly to every help-oriented contact between two people, even if it is called *pastoral* counseling. We say this because some pastors refer to all helping contacts with people as counseling. By this usage even unplanned contacts and telephone conversations are called counseling if some effort at helping another person ensues. The meaning of words is, of course, arbitrary, but the author would argue that the word *counseling* should be given technical status. A differentiation between pastoral counseling and pastoral care should be made.

The distinction is this: The word *counseling* applies best only to situations where (1) two persons have knowingly entered into a relationship, (2) in which one attempts to help the other, and (3) where an established series of meetings is arranged for this purpose. *Pastoral care* is a broader term. It covers all helping contacts between pastor and people. Pastoral care includes such activities as one-time "counseling," visiting the sick, attending the dying, comforting the bereaved, and administering the sacraments. *Pastoral counseling* is a specific type of activity, a subcategory, within the broad area of pastoral care.

Pastoral counseling involves a decision to deal with an individual to alleviate his distress in a particular way. This brings the term into line with accepted usage of the term *counseling* in the mental health professions. It also makes possible certain additional distinctions noted below, but first perhaps an example will help clarify the distinction. Suppose a pastor has a telephone call from a person in distress. If he offers his help, sooner or later he is going to have a decision to make. Will he offer the individual a sustained series of counseling sessions? Or will he meet him only once or twice to see what he can do to help him? The pastor may not know the answer to this question at the time of the telephone call, but eventually he will do one or the other. If he has no expectation that the man will be back or if he makes no move toward setting up a continuing relationship, he is providing pastoral care. It will be less misleading if he does not refer to this as counseling. On the other hand, if he meets the telephone caller and after an initial conversation or two they agree to meet once a week for an hour to explore the person's problem, this is counseling.

There are other differences between pastoral care and pastoral counseling. One is that pastoral care usually aims to provide rapid solution for a problem or alleviate immediate distress, and in this sense it is *situation* oriented. Pastoral counseling involves a more prolonged contact, and immediate solution of the problem is not expected. Counseling seeks not only to solve a problem or remove distress but to alter, if possible, the psychological conditions that produced it. This usually requires slow exploration of the problem and of related problems and of problems behind problems. Counseling attempts to help the person think differently and feel differently about a whole area or several areas of his life. It can even happen that at the end of counseling the specific problem remains because it is essentially insoluble, but the person feels differently about it. He feels capable of coping with it.

Still another difference between pastoral care and pastoral

counseling lies in the directness of the application of God's Word. In pastoral care Biblical precepts are usually brought quickly and immediately into the relationship by the pastor. In pastoral counseling, while concern for the person's spiritual welfare is not hidden or relinquished, it is not necessarily drawn immediately into the conversation *by the pastor.* The person is there to work out his problems. It is hoped, if he is a Christian, that he will make his own applications of God's Word to his situation. Direct confrontation of the person with God's Word at the instigation of the pastor will come much later in the counseling relationship, if it is necessary at all.

When the kinds of situations the pastor typically meets are examined, it turns out that some of them call for pastoral care; some permit either pastoral care or pastoral counseling; some indicate that pastoral counseling definitely is needed; and some indicate that the services of another profession are required. Take some examples. When the pastor calls on unchurched people, he is involved in pastoral care. He speaks the Word as clearly and as effectively as he can. Usually when he calls on the sick, the dying, the bereaved, he is providing pastoral care. However, not always. It is conceivable that he might also offer a bereaved widower a series of counseling sessions to explore his reactions to his wife's death. He might offer the same to the surgery patient or even the terminal cancer patient, but usually he would not.

In marriage problems, vocational choice problems, adolescent behavior problems, he could provide either pastoral care or pastoral counseling. When pastoral care is the choice, it is often in the nature of patching or troubleshooting. For example, he tries to effect a reconciliation of the embattled couple. In that context he may speak the Law to the husband, telling him his duty before God. He may use the Gospel with the wife, urging her to be as forgiving as Christ. In a vocational problem, he may suggest educational alternatives to a person or ask a congregation member to help the person find a job. On the other hand, in most of these situations pastoral counseling could be offered instead. The pastor could agree to meet regularly with the husband and wife, either separately or jointly, to explore the causes of their marital discord. In a vocational problem he could offer to meet regularly with a person to help him decide for himself what he wants to do in life.

In other instances, for example when a person exhibits chronic worry or unexplained anxiety or constant difficulty in getting along with people, a counseling relationship seems clearly indicated. Finally, when the pastor thinks the problem lies beyond his competence, referral elsewhere is needed.

Every pastor is committed by his office to providing pastoral care in a variety of situations. The question a pastor ought to answer for himself is whether or not, in addition, he intends and is competent to do pastoral counseling. Pastoral care he must provide, often on a crash basis, but he should undertake to do counseling only after deliberation and a specific decision.

Permissive and Directive Attitudes

A third major decision the pastor ought to make deliberately is whether he will take a *permissive* or *directive* role in counseling, or some mixture thereof.

Permissiveness and directiveness in attitude are not discrete alternatives. They are ends of a continuum. Taking a permissive role means to adopt an attitude that allows the person a large or even an unlimited degree of latitude in making decisions about his life. The counselor exerts little or no effort to induce the person to adopt a particular point of view about himself or to follow a particular line of action. Taking a directive role, on the other hand, refers to an approach in which the counselor believes he knows what is best for the person and attempts to get him to accept this viewpoint.

The client-centered approach of Carl Rogers represents a relatively extreme form of the permissive approach in counseling. The methods of some authority-oriented counselors in persuading and "reasoning" with people to get them "to do the right thing" are examples of the directive approach.

Being directive is not necessarily synonymous with poor counseling, but it has serious hazards. Part of the difficulty lies in the fact that being directive involves giving advice, offering explanations, telling the person what to do and how to think. In many people's past such an approach has too often been associated with worthless counsel and painful coercion. It arouses fears of further manipulation and interferes with the counseling process. Another part of the difficulty lies in the fact that counselors who take a directive approach are tempted to reject the person when their explanations and solutions are not accepted. They tend to interpret a counselee's failure to accept their views as willful noncompliance, when it is usually inability to believe or do what is expected. Under such conditions, counseling is unlikely to get very far.

The pastor needs to answer for himself how permissive he can be. His, by tradition, is not a permissive occupation. The history of pastoral care, at least until very recently, has leaned more toward telling people what to think and do than toward letting them work it out for themselves. By contrast, good counseling is characterized by willingness to let people work out for themselves the solutions to their problems. The counselor acts more as a catalyst, which facilitates the problem-solving process, than as a reactive agent which determines the nature of the end product.

It is perhaps clear that the author thinks a basically permissive stance is necessary for pastoral counseling. However, some extremely important, even painful, issues arise if such a stance is adopted. But before looking further at some of these issues, we need to make two things clear:

First, *for the next three chapters we will be talking primarily about pastoral counseling.* We will have occasion to make side references to pastoral care, but the main concern will be with sustained counseling relationships.

Second, the author's view of what pastoral counseling is is this:

1. Pastoral counseling is essentially a *relationship* in which the pastor attempts to help a person in distress by providing a permissive atmosphere in which that person can experience himself more completely and find solutions to his problems.

2. Pastoral counseling requires a great deal *more listening* and a good deal *less telling* than untrained counselors normally employ.

3. A good place to begin counseling is with the client-centered approach of *responding to the feelings and perceptions* expressed by the person, but that is *not* the place to end one's approach.

4. Pastoral counseling permits a limited amount of *interpretation,* if this is handled wisely. It may also require *confrontation,* a concept to be defined shortly.

Now we can return to our discussion of permissiveness and directiveness.

A stance somewhere between absolute permissiveness (if such is really possible) and normal directiveness is required in pastoral counseling. The very enterprise of counseling, if it is to get anywhere, requires the counselor to be less directive than people ordinarily are in their relations with each other. Certainly it requires the pastor to be less directive than does pastoral care. On the other hand, the pastor's basic objective and his responsibility to the Gospel place a requirement on him also. His objective and his responsibility do not permit him to renounce completely all rights to express his own ideas about what is best for the person or what God's Word says or what the implications of a person's decisions or actions are.

The place to start, therefore, is with letting the person express aloud his own thoughts concerning his problem, his feelings, his wishes, and his actions. The pastor's initial task is to try to gain empathic understanding of that world, the one in which the person really lives. His task is to convey, also aloud, what he understands the person to be saying about his inner experience. Such reflection of feelings and perceptions accomplishes two ends. It conveys to the person that the pastor is an individual who can and will try to understand him. And it helps the person see and hear more clearly what his thoughts and feelings really are.

The last is not a minor matter, because it turns out that thoughts spoken only to one's self do not seem and sound quite the same when they are spoken out loud. Furthermore, when they are reflected back by a counselor, they take on still another dimension. Out of such changed perspectives of one's thoughts and feelings come changes in self-concept and behavior. The counselor aids this process by deliberately setting out to respond to and reflect back the person's own thoughts and feelings. (How to do that is taken up in Chapter 4.) Imbedded in such an approach is a basic permissiveness that gives the person opportunity to work through his experiences and problems in a safe atmosphere.

In what sense and when may the pastor become directive? Generally speaking, he should not become directive, if ever, until well along in the counseling process. To be more specific, he should not become directive until (1) a deep sense of rapport and trust has developed between the person and the counselor and (2) the person has had adequate chance to explore his problems in his own way and at his own pace. Usually this will be a matter of several counseling hours at least, and it may be a matter of months.

Confrontation

There is a specific sense in which the pastor as a counselor may sometimes become more directive. To describe the sense in which the pastor may legitimately become directive in counseling, the author has chosen the word *confrontation*. By confrontation is meant just that—confronting the person with some aspect of himself in relation to God's will for men. For example, it may be a matter of confronting the individual with the fact that, although he has talked about his vocational-choice difficulties for several counseling hours, this has always been from the viewpoint of how much *he* would like various kinds of work, how much *he* would earn, how much prestige and security *he* would have in various occupations. He has not considered which occupation would give him the greatest opportunity to serve God and his fellowman; he has not considered earning power as a means to an end rather than as an end in itself; he has not asked himself in what way he might use the talents God has given him or what God's will for him might be.

It might be a matter of confronting a couple who have come for marital counseling with the fact that in several counseling sessions they have talked about what they do not like about each other; they have aired old grievances; they have even kissed and made up. But they have not asked themselves what a Christian marriage is; they have not explored the relationship of Christ's love for them to their love for each other. They have talked about sex, but they have not seen sex in its Christian perspective. They have talked about their children but not their responsibilities as parents.

Confrontation is not accusation. It is done with a different spirit. Accusation is meant to hurt, to make a person feel bad. Confrontation is done in a calm and quiet manner. Its purpose is to make the person think. It is the raising of a question, not the demanding of an answer. Confrontation has within it the danger that it may be misunderstood as an accusation or as a blow meant to hurt. Consequently, it must be carried out with the same careful skill with which the surgeon uses his scalpel or the artist his brush. It must not be done prematurely. The person must be given sufficient opportunity to explore his problems and come upon their spiritual implications by himself. Confrontation requires judgment on the pastor's part—judgment as to how deep a sense of trust the distressed person has developed toward the pastor and how strong the feeling of the distressed person is that the pastor does not mean to hurt him. No arbitrary rule can be laid down, but generally speaking it should be late in counseling. (Confrontation is dealt with again in detail in Chapter 5.)

Justification for such an approach, if it is needed, can probably be found even in the client-centered counseling approach. The client-centered people acknowledge that when something about the client or what he intends to do becomes of such deep concern to the counselor that it bothers him seriously, the matter had better be dealt with openly. The reason is that the counselor is not "congruent" if something about the counseling relationship is of deep concern to him and yet is kept hidden. Such incongruence can impair the counseling relationship.

It might happen in client-centered counseling, for example, that the client is planning to take a step the counselor feels will be seriously detrimental. If the stress continues, the counselor will bring up his concern with the client—not with the intention of manipulating the client into taking a different path but to get the therapist's concerns out in the open. The issue is broached in a truly permissive manner; the client is still free to make his own decision. But the counselor's concern is also disclosed and can be dealt with by both client and counselor.

The relevance of this to pastoral counseling is this. The

pastor may also develop internal stresses with respect to a person he is counseling, and it is important that they not be allowed to fester inside him. He is particularly likely to become concerned about the person's spiritual welfare, specifically about his Christian faith and life. As counseling proceeds, if the distressed person fails to relate his life and problems to these spiritual concerns, the pastor's internal stress increases. At the point where it begins to look as if the person will never get around to relating himself to God's Word, the pastor's stress may require him to confront the individual.

Thus the pastor is not totally permissive in his counseling. He does not relinquish the right to bring into the counseling relationship those issues that are of ultimate spiritual concern to himself and to the individual. He attempts to achieve those aspects of his objectives that are unique to his profession, and in this way he is true to his calling as a Christian pastor. The Word of God and the Gospel of Jesus Christ ultimately get into the counseling relationship. Preferably this is when the person spontaneously talks about his relationship to God, but if not on the person's initiative, then on the pastor's initiative.

The pastor, according to this viewpoint, is *not* directive in his counseling in a different sense, however. While he is free to bring up the individual's relation to God, he is not free to become manipulative with God's Word. He is not free to use God's Word to bludgeon a person into some type of compliance. Offering to enter into a counseling relationship of the type we are discussing involves the pastor in an implicit commitment not to become manipulative and certainly not to become coercive. In counseling there is an honest agreement to let a person find his own answers and choose his own outcomes. If the pastor is unwilling to make this commitment, he had better reject this type of counseling. To repeat, in this approach to counseling the pastor retains the right to bring issues into counseling for consideration. He relinquishes the right to become manipulative, argumentative, coercive, or judgmental.

A word of warning is needed! Responding to and reflecting feelings and perceptions convey to a person a certain kind of permissiveness about the counseling relationship. It says to the person that it is all right to go on exploring himself, and it is all right to come to his own decisions. The pastor cannot change horses in the middle of the stream. The pastor-counselor must not lead a person on with a permissive attitude if he is likely to turn on the person and become judgmental or coercive when the person mentions experiences or makes decisions that alarm the counselor because they do not fit his ideas of what a Christian should be like. The result of such a change of manner on the part of the counselor can be catastrophic. The person feels threatened and betrayed. Not only may this ruin the counseling relationship, it may prevent the person from ever seeking counseling from anyone again, because it becomes one more in a series of disappointments and betrayals by other human beings. In some cases the letdown may precipitate a severe mental disorder, and it would have been better if the pastor had never begun counseling.

To cite examples, the pastor may find it easy to reflect feeling and be permissive when an adolescent is exploring the hurts and humiliations of childhood; it may be much more difficult to do so when the same adolescent contemplates a course of action contrary to conventional moral norms. The pastor may find it easy to be nondirective when a man ruminates about dissatisfactions in his marriage; it will be much harder when the man contemplates divorce or an extramarital affair. Probably the greatest test of the pastor's ability to let another person find his own answers will be when he encounters someone who decides to give up church membership or even his Christian commitment. If under these circumstances the pastor suddenly changes direction and begins to suggest that the person is a bad person for having such thoughts, or if he implies by word or action that he will no longer accept the person with unconditional positive regard if he persists in carrying out these intentions, then the person who came for help is in great danger. And the danger is not only danger with respect to his emotional health. The danger involves the person's spiritual welfare in the deepest sense. Betrayal by a pastor is serious business!

But decisions to engage in behavior that God's Word condemns or a decision to abandon one's Christian commitment are also serious business, of course. They raise the question, Can the pastor appear to condone such behavior and such decisions by remaining permissive and unconditionally accepting? There are several possible answers. One is that the pastor may have no other choice. The person is going to reject Christianity or pursue his intended course of action no matter what the pastor does. If the pastor responds with nonaccepting and manipulative responses, he merely speeds up the undesired outcome.

Second, it is not true that if a pastor responds by reflecting feeling and showing understanding and acceptance, he thereby also condones the contemplated decision or the behavior. If the pastor does not immediately begin to coax, coerce, persuade, or in some way talk the person out of his intended behavior, he does not thereby approve of it. Someone might reason that his silence constitutes tacit approval. But is this really so? An accepting attitude is not necessarily an approving attitude. For example, if a person describes his anxiety and the pastor responds sensitively to that feeling, the pastor is not thereby saying that it is fine to have anxiety. Nor is he saying in this instance that it would be fine to give up one's Christianity or to continue an unacceptable pattern of behavior.

Third, people ought to have the right to bow out of Christianity without being intimidated. Confronted with what they are doing? Yes! Confronted with the seriousness of their action? Certainly! But intimidated? Threatened? Manipulated with emotional arguments? No! One of the great difficulties of the Christian church lies in the fact that for many of its adherents not being a Christian has never been a live option. They are Christian (perhaps one should only say they are church members) by upbringing, by habit, or because they do not want to disappoint parents, spouse, or pastor. But they have never really chosen Christianity; they just slid into it.

In the course of counseling, when a person reexamines his Christian commitment or his commitment to conventional moral patterns, he may discover his own shallowness. He may decide it is time for a change. At these times it may be difficult for the pastor to maintain his permissive stance. But if he has decided to take such a stance, he cannot legitimately abandon it when the going gets rough. He must be particularly careful that he is not confusing his own problems about Christian commitment and morality with those of the person he is counseling. He may be inclined to panic over what the person is contemplating, because it lies so close to his own temptations. Thus the pastor's own openness about himself (congruence) becomes critical. But the point here is that counseling must involve a genuinely safe situation in which a person can work out his problems. The pastor reserves the right to confront the individual with the implications of his problem and his decisions, but he relinquishes the right to become manipulative.

Finally, some points about persons who consider abandoning Christianity or continuing in a manifestly sinful behavior pattern are these: Some of what people talk about in counseling is more in the realm of phantasy than action. It can even happen that what a person describes as accomplished fact is really only what he wishes he could do. In counseling, people work out their fears and hopes and dreams. They also test them out at the level of talk rather than action.

The matter can be even more complex, however. If it is assumed that counseling provides a safe place to explore one's self and that the past experiences of most people make them wary of exposing themselves, it is likely that the person will *test out* the safety of the situation. The person will put forth some thought, some wish, some past experience that seems shocking or to which pastors are "supposed" to object, to see how the pastor takes it. The person tests to see whether or not the situation is really as safe as it seems. If the pastor reacts with shock or with manipulation, that tells the person where he stands. If the pastor reacts with acceptance and understanding, the person is relieved. He can proceed.

Testing out can happen repeatedly. As the person approaches something painful and important but something he is not sure the pastor will be able to accept, the testing may occur again. The person begins to edge toward the problem, but first he puts out some material designed to reassure himself that he is not going to be hurt if he talks about the really significant problem. This constant need to test the situation goes on to some extent in every counseling relationship, sometimes up to the very end of counseling.

The pastor also has to consider that what the distressed person will use to test him out is partly determined by the fact that he is a pastor. The two points on which a pastor can be expected to get excited and become defensive or manipulative are Christian commitment and sin. By profession the pastor is supposed to be *for* Christian commitment (often defined as church membership) and *against* sin (sometimes confused with social conventions). If a person needs to test out, these are the areas most likely to be chosen, and they are likely to be chosen unconsciously.

A word of hope and comfort can even be offered to the pastor-counselor. The chances are excellent that the person will finally resolve his problem in the direction of Christian commitment and acceptable Christian morality — not inevitable, but excellent. Most times the person really needs only to go through a symbolic separation from the church or a symbolic moral revolt so that he or she can be truly free to accept Christianity and its moral code. Then the person can feel that his choice comes from internal conviction rather than external pressure. In brief, the person, being free not to be a Christian or free to be immoral, is also, for the first time, really free to be a Christian or to be moral. When this happens, the person feels keenly that his decision is no longer one of compulsion but one of choice. It is a moving experience to see this happening in counseling. The counselor is watching the spiritual growth of a human being take place right before his eyes.

4

Responding to Feelings and Perceptions

In this chapter we examine in some detail what it means to respond to and reflect a person's feelings and perceptions in counseling. In a sense, this kind of responding on the part of the pastor-counselor constitutes the basic work of counseling. It is the primary activity of the counselor.

There are three parts in what follows: the first part deals with the rationale of reflecting feelings and perceptions. The second part gives some suggestions as to how to go about this kind of responding, using a made-up counseling situation for purposes of illustration. In the third part exerpts from actual counseling responses are used to illustrate what happens in this type of counseling.

The Responses of the Counselor

When a person comes to a professional counselor, he wants help with his problems. Whether he gets help will depend on how the counselor *responds* to him. Counseling may be thought of as a two-way interaction. First the person says something about himself, and then the counselor replies. In the terminology of counseling, the counselor's reply is a *response*. What the person says or does next will depend greatly on the counselor's response. This view of the counseling conversation as a series of interrelated responses is the key idea in what follows.

How a counselor responds in counseling is probably much

more important than the theory of personality a counselor holds or how he thinks people become emotionally distressed in the first place. It is possible to state with some clarity what constitute good types of responses for counselors to make and what constitute poor responses. If the counselor responds in certain ways, the person will feel safe. He will go on exploring his problems. He will ventilate his feelings. He will move toward a better understanding of himself. He will feel better about his problems, and he will probably find better ways of handling them. If the counselor responds in certain other ways, the person will become anxious, threatened, defensive. The person will find it difficult to go on, and it is extremely likely that he will *not* achieve a better understanding of himself or find better ways of dealing with his problems. He may terminate counseling prematurely.

What kinds of counselor responses impede counseling? (1) Responses that *probe* and dig around by asking questions.[5] (2) Responses that *judge* a person by labeling his thoughts or behavior good, bad, nice, foolish, and the like. (3) Responses that try to *reassure, comfort,* or *console* the person by trying to talk him out of feeling the way he does. (4) Responses that try to explain or *interpret* to the person the reasons behind his feelings. (5) Responses that *give advice,* that is, tell the person how to feel or what to do. Each of these kinds of responses is likely to impede counseling for a different reason. *Probing* responses may frighten a person if he is not ready to reveal himself. *Judging* responses may make the person feel guilty or worthless, feelings he is trying to avoid. *Reassuring* responses usually offer "cheap" or "hollow" comfort. While the person may feel temporarily relieved, this usually does not last. *Interpretive* responses usually cannot be assimilated by the person, and often they too threaten him. *Advice* is easy to give but hard to use, and most people have had more than enough well-meant advice.

What kinds of responses facilitate counseling? (1) Responses that catch the *feelings* a person is experiencing and reflect them back. (2) Responses that capture the person's *perceptions* of himself and his situation and reflect them back. Good counselor responses *reflect* back the person's feelings and perceptions, that is, his *experience* with himself and his situation. The term *reflect* implies that the counselor puts what the person is feeling and perceiving into words. It is a way of recognizing and clarifying the person's experiences. The counselor determines what the person is feeling and experiencing from what the person *says* and from *behavioral cues* like facial expression, body position, and tone of voice. Responses that reflect feelings and perceptions facilitate counseling because they promote a safe feeling in the person. They show that the counselor *understands* the person and *accepts* him. In this safe atmosphere the person finds that he is really free to explore himself and find answers to his problems. In addition, counselor responses that accurately reflect what the person is experiencing help the person understand his experiences better. Often they let him see himself in a new light. From such understanding can come a changed self-concept and altered behavior.

Responding to Feelings and Perceptions

The big question, of course, is how to help a counselor learn to respond to feelings and perceptions and reflect them back to the person being counseled. It is not certain to what extent learning to respond appropriately in counseling can be conveyed through a book. However, we can suggest (1) a general attitude or point of view for the counselor to take and (2) a few "tricks of the trade" he can use in getting started.

Previously we noted that to reflect feelings and perceptions is to put them into words for the person. To do this requires the counselor to adopt a specific attitude. Basically the counselor has to keep asking himself: "What is this person feeling?" "What is this person experiencing?" "How does the problem look to him?" The counselor has to be constantly alert to clues that will identify what the person is experiencing. The clues are many and varied. Sometimes it is what the person *says* — "I'm afraid I may be losing my mind." Sometimes it is the *way* the person says it — slowly, sadly, angrily, or happily. Sometimes it is a *facial expression* — a look of disgust, a smile, the flush of embarrassment. Sometimes it is *posture* — sitting tensely on the edge of the chair, slouching in a dejected heap.

A few specific aids can be suggested to help the counselor focus on feelings and perceptions. A word of warning must be given, however: *These aids must not become mere cliches!*

One set of aids consists of words designed to *make* the counselor focus on feelings and perceptions. Examples are: "You feel that . . . ." "It seems to you . . . ." "I hear you saying . . . ." "The way you saw it . . . ." Note that by their nature these expressions require the counselor to finish the sentence with a reflection of feelings or perceptions. The hazard is that if they are used as a "gimmick," the counselor may create fictional feelings and perceptions just to complete the sentence. Clearly, the counselor must wait until he has adequate grounds for making a statement of what the person appears to be experiencing.

The last statement raises the question of what the counselor does when he is not sure what experience the person is expressing. That is often the case in counseling. It is one reason why good counselors listen a lot and talk relatively little. Fortunately, there are also aids to keep the person talking so that his feelings and perceptions will become apparent. One is simply to say nothing at all. Silence requires the person to keep talking, since most people try to keep conversation going. The only trouble is that silence can also be very threatening. Most people, including counselors until they become experienced, are made uncomfortable by silence. Another procedure is for the counselor to reply, "Mmh hmn," to the person's statements. This is done in a "Yes, I'm trying to understand — keep going" tone. A third approach is simply to tell the person: "I'm not sure I understand how you feel about that," or "I'm not sure I know how you see this situation." Obviously, variants on these expressions are in order. All responses should fit the counselor's usual manner of speaking. His exact words are unimportant. The critical point is that the counselor shows he wants to understand what the person is experiencing.

Finally, when the counselor believes he understands something of what the person is experiencing, he reflects this back to the person. Usually, but not always, this is done with words. Sometimes it is enough simply to nod affirmatively or say, "Mmh hmn," this time in an "I understand" tone. Use of a nod or "Mmh hmn" is particularly in order when the counselor has just reflected the feeling or perception of the person, and the person is now expanding on that experience or exploring it further.

The next section is in programed-learning format. It is based on the preceding sections. To use the "program," read the frames on the right and try to fill in the blank or answer the question. If necessary, go back to the text. Suggested answers are in the left-hand frames below the questions. Cover the answers until you are ready to check yourself. Getting the exact words is not, of course, important.

COUNSELOR: "Your thoughts really disturb you at times."
PERSON: "Sometimes I think I must be a terrible person. Only a person with a depraved mind could think such things."

In order to formulate his next response, the counselor ought to adopt the attitude that asks: "What is this person _____?"

feeling or
experiencing

Look at the person's last statement again. The key words are "terrible person" and "depraved mind." What *feelings* do you believe are being expressed? (1) anger, (2) joy, (3) self-disparagement, (4) fear.

(3)

PERSON (continuing): "I mean, where could these thoughts come from? I don't want to think them. They just come into my head. . . . And that's why I can't sleep." (Said while clenching hands)

In addition to asking what this person is feeling or experiencing, the counselor should also ask himself: "How does she see _____?"

herself or the
situation

How *does* the person see herself? (1) absolutely hopeless, (2) unable to control her thoughts, (3) her thoughts caused by lack of sleep, (4) hopeful of a solution.

(2)

In the person's last response (above), there is a *nonverbal* clue to how she feels.

a. The clue comes in the form of
_____ _____.

b. From the information given would you estimate that the person experiences her problem mildly or rather intensely?

clenched hands
intensely

COUNSELOR: "You feel unable to control these thoughts that bother you so."

What words in the counselor's response are designed to *make* him focus on the person's *feelings?*

"You feel"

COUNSELOR: "As you see it, you can't sleep because you can't control these bothersome thoughts."

What words in the counselor's response show that he is trying to focus on the person's *perceptions* of herself?

"As you *see* it"

PERSON: "Oh! It's terrible. I toss and turn. I feel so . . . so . . . so . . . ugly. Maybe I should just be put away."
COUNSELOR: "It seems to you that you must be an awful person."

Now what words does the counselor use to make himself focus on her feelings and perceptions?

"It seems to you"

PERSON: "Well, if you wished your husband were dead, wouldn't you think it was pretty awful? There now! I've said it."
COUNSELOR: "I hear you saying you expect me to think you're awful too."

What words help him catch her feeling and perceptions now?

"I hear you saying"

PERSON: (Crying) "Oh, I don't know what to do . . . (sob) . . . what to do. Can anything help me, Pastor? Am I hopeless?"

COUNSELOR: "_____" (Start the counselor's response with words that will make him focus on feelings or perception.)

"You feel," "It seems to you," etc.

COUNSELOR: "You feel pretty upset about these thoughts."

PERSON: "They scare me something awful. They must mean something. I must be losing my mind if I can think such things."

COUNSELOR: "You are _____ by your thoughts." (Supply a word to reflect *feeling*.)

frightened

PERSON: (Long pause) "I love John. I really do. I don't know what gets into me . . . what puts these thoughts into my head. I'm so mixed up. Oh, I don't know what to do!"

The person's expression of feelings now shifts away from fear to a feeling of _____.

confusion or helplessness

COUNSELOR: "_____" (Compose an entire counselor response that will reflect the feeling just identified.

Begin with a phrase designed to *make* the counselor focus on feelings and perceptions.)

"You feel confused."
"You feel helpless to control your thoughts."

PERSON: "Well, yes. I do love John. I'd do anything for him. But then . . . at night . . . I have these thoughts about what it would be like if . . . if . . . I can't say it again. It's just too awful to talk about." (Lowers her eyes and hangs head)

COUNSELOR: "We all have bothersome thoughts at times."

Is the counselor trying to be helpful? Is this kind of response really likely to help?

Your opinion! (The author thinks not.)

PERSON: (Continuing) "I guess I must be just about the most awful person you ever met."

COUNSELOR: "As you see it, you _____"

(Complete the response so it will reflect how she *sees* herself.)

"are a terrible person."

But if the person's feelings and perceptions were not so apparent, the counselor would use a response to keep the person talking until she revealed her inner experience. Three suggested aids were: (1) Say _____ at all. (2) Nod affirmatively or say: "_____." (3) Say: "I'm not sure I understand how _____"

nothing

PERSON: "Yes, I guess I do feel like a

"Mmh hmn"
"you feel about
that" or "you see
the situation."

terrible person. But John is no saint either. Living with him all these years has been trying. Some ways John is the finest person that ever lived. But he's completely thoughtless at times."

COUNSELOR: "_____" (Supply a response to keep the person talking.)

One of the
responses above.

PERSON: "He never tells me when he'll be home. He never tells me he loves me or shows any appreciation for all I do for him. Sometimes I feel like a doormat. Like a servant."

Would you agree that the counselor's last response kept the person talking and helped reveal the person's perception of the situation?

Your opinion!

1. Of the suggested aids for keeping a person talking so that he reveals his inner experience, which one says to the person, "Yes, yes, I'm trying to understand. Keep going"?
2. Which one is a frank admission that the counselor isn't sure he understands but really wants to understand?

Affirmative nod, or
"Mmh hmn."
"I'm not sure
I understand
how _____"

1. Which kind of response forces the person to keep talking because most people need to keep a conversation going?
2. The use of silence can be hazardous,

however, because it makes the person feel _____.

Saying nothing, uncomfortable or threatened

When the counselor believes he has caught the person's feelings or his perception of the situation, he should reflect this back to the person. But if the counselor has just reflected a feeling or perception and an elaboration or further exploration follows, it may be enough to nod or say "_____ _____" in an "I understand" tone.

"Mmh hmn"

PERSON: "I guess I really feel two ways about John. I love him. But I hate some of his ways. I don't think I've ever admitted that before."

COUNSELOR: "_____" (Supply a response that will encourage the person to continue to explore her ambivalent feelings of love and hate.)

Nod, say nothing, "Mmh hmn," etc.

PERSON: "It's strange. I have these two feelings about John. I love him, and I detest him. It's like I could never admit his faults before. You know, it's kind of a relief to have it out in the open. . . . It sure is. . . . Kind of a relief. Like I don't have to hide it."

Would you say that she is continuing to explore herself?

Your opinion!

PERSON: "It sure is a relief to say it out loud . . . not to have to keep it inside."

COUNSELOR: "_____" (Compose a response to reflect the person's dominant feeling.)

"You feel relieved now that it's out."

PERSON: (Breathing deeply and exhaling) "Yes . . . Yes . . . I can admit it for the first time. After all these years of putting on a show of perfect devotion. My . . . my . . ."

This growing awareness of ambivalent feelings and the ability to face them is partly what is meant by "progress" in counseling. As we shall see in Chapter 5, *ambivalence* is at the core of many emotional problems.

Examples from Actual Counseling Situations

There can be in life a wide difference between theory and practice or between what a person says he does and what actually transpires. Counseling is no exception. In the following excerpts from actual counseling interactions we see representative responses of a counselor to people's feelings and perceptions. The reader can judge for himself how well theory fits practice. We note the large proportion of talk by the person compared to that by the counselor. We note also that many statements by the person being counseled contain more than one distinct element. The counselor could choose to respond to one or another of them. Usually he chooses the feeling or perception that appears dominant or to one that continues to develop a theme that has already been started. Sometimes, however, he will pick a new element that he feels is an important one for the person to explore further.

The first counseling excerpt is from the 10th session with a young man who came with a vocational-choice problem. The son of a clergyman, he was a student in a church-related college, preparing to enter a theological seminary. As he came nearer to graduation from college and the change to the seminary, two things began to happen. One was that, although he was a capable student and had previously had adequate grades, he began to do poorly in his studies and had nearly failed a course in the previous term. The other was that he began to feel extremely uncomfortable in church services. In church and chapel his anxiety rose to a near panic state. These were the complaints, but it developed in counseling that the real problem behind them was whether he wanted to be a minister, and behind that was a problem of becoming independent from his parents and being able to make his own decisions. As soon as this was openly acknowledged, the anxiety about attending church subsided considerably, and he reported that he was able to study better.

The excerpt was selected to show how responding to a person's feelings and perceptions permits him to explore himself and arrive at his own conclusions.

PERSON: Well, I've been struggling to try and see things as clearly as I can. It's not too easy to do. But let's say first, in the line of vocation, I guess somehow I've always had the idea that, let's say, if you had the ability to be a minister and you didn't, you weren't doing all that you could do. In other words, saving souls would be more desirable than some other form of work. I mean, you'd be better in God's sight or something than in any other line of work. Let's say, if you had the ability to do it.

COUNSELOR: You felt anybody with the right amount of

intelligence and other attributes was, in a sense, obligated to be a minister.

PERSON: That if you weren't, you weren't doing all that you could for God. In other words, I feel a Christian should make the best use of his life for God. But, I mean, since we're an individual, it just seems like we ought to take that into consideration too. 'Cause there are certainly many men who have the intelligence and the ability to be ministers that just don't want to be, I suppose. I don't know how else you'd put it. Well, let's put it this way. They might like another type of work better. I don't know; I've always had the idea that with ministers you were witnessing more than you could in any other way. But I don't know; I'm beginning to think more and more that this isn't true.

COUNSELOR: You are starting to think differently.

PERSON: Right. That the ministry in a sense, I mean, in a sense a pastor is simply a Christian among Christians, and he really isn't any better than they are. It's just that he enjoys this particular type of work more than someone else would. Now maybe this is wrong, but this is the way it's beginning to seem to me. That he might enjoy working with a Bible class or Sunday school or the church service itself and all the normal everyday activities of people in the church. Maybe I don't have the right idea of it, but . . . (Voice trails off)

COUNSELOR: I wonder if you're not saying: "Sometimes I feel it's pretty important for a person to be happy in his work."

Here the counselor could have responded either to his feeling that it's important to like one's work or to his misgivings about asserting his own ideas. He chose the former.

PERSON: What I'm very interested in finding is some vocation where I can feel like I'm doing something that I really enjoy doing. Maybe I'll never find this, but it seems to me this is possible. Some people just might be more prone to enjoy the workings of a congregation more than other people. I'm trying to look at myself as an individual . . . doing what he enjoys doing . . . rather than doing what he feels he ought to do. Or rather, trying to somehow combine the two anyway. I don't know if I'm saying it very clearly.

COUNSELOR: One of the things I hear you saying is: "There are things about the ministry that don't appeal too much to me."

PERSON: Yeah, I just don't know if I could. Granted, the only real experience I've had is in my own church. You know, seeing how this particular church operates, and what activities they do, and the pastor's role in these. Somehow, I just don't know . . . I don't know . . . whether I could do that.

In this session the student went on to explore his ambivalence about the ministry. This led in subsequent sessions to a realization that much of his conflict derived from certain other questions. One was whether a person can be himself in the ministry or whether one has to put on a false front and hide his real self. Part of this came from his image of his father, whom he saw as being a much different person in public than he was at home. He eventually came to the conclusion that in any vocation he might choose he would have problems about being his "true self," as he called it. The ministry, he decided, might be somewhat more restrictive than other vocations but not enough to make a critical difference for him.

He also explored what it meant to make his own vocational choice and resist what he thought was his father's wish that he enter the ministry. In the course of this exploration there was a period in which he was firmly convinced that he would not enter the ministry. The counselor saw this as a symbolic way of declaring his independence from father. During this time the student reexamined his father's oft-made statement that he should make his own decision.

To indicate how this person experienced himself at a later time and how he had become more honest and open (congruent), here is an excerpt from a later counseling session.

PERSON: Well, I think I'm finally getting someplace. I was talking to my dad. Just finally decided to come out and tell him that some things were really bugging me, that I just had to be more honest with myself and with them. Just, you know, came out and told them that for all these years what has been botherin' me, at least what I *think* has been botherin' me, is the tension of being something or trying to be something that I'm not. I think what I was doing is I was trying to do something and yet to run away from it at the same time. I was trying to have a strong Christian faith, and yet I was trying to do lots of other things. And somehow all these things just didn't work, and . . . ah . . . I guess I can see now a lot of my problem was that I felt so guilty . . . so I just told my dad all about this, and I told him, you know, that I couldn't lead my life for his sake or anyone else's, any more than he could for his father's sake or for his wife's sake or anything like that. He told me that the only way I was ever going to be happy was to be honest with myself.

COUNSELOR: So you got a favorable response from him.

PERSON: I figured I would, but somehow doing it and getting it out relieves a lot of the tension. I don't know exactly why, but it feels different.

The next excerpt is from a session with an unmarried woman in her early thirties who lived with her mother. They did not get along well, and the daughter felt her life was dominated by her mother. She was very unhappy about this situation, but she had been unable to do anything about it. The excerpt is included to show how the counselor might employ open admission that he doesn't fully understand a person's experience in order to facilitate the self-exploration process.

The woman has just been talking about the way in which her mother constantly accuses her of deliberately trying to hurt her feelings.

COUNSELOR: I'm not sure I know how you feel when she attacks you, when, as you see it, you haven't meant any harm.

PERSON: Well, I have two ways. One, I become angry. And two, I think she's some kind of nut. In a way I . . . I think she could use psychological help quite a bit herself. I mean, I don't want to be a handy-dandy home analyst or something, but some of these things . . . . She's quite a bit overweight, and the doctor suggests that she go on a diet. And so she'll avoid going to see the doctor because she doesn't want to be told the same thing again. Oh, any number of things — taking my things, misperceiving what I consider reality, and things like this . . . .

COUNSELOR: I gather that you would be very reluctant to suggest to her that she might need some psychological help.

> The counselor here ignored her reference to anger in favor of what was essentially a new issue, the possibility her mother needs help too. Which is the more critical question for her becomes apparent in the subsequent responses.

PERSON: I'd be afraid of drawing some more fire. I think if I did . . . I don't think it would do any good, really, because I'm pretty sure she wouldn't go. And if she went once or twice, she'd quit soon afterwards anyway. She, uh . . . well, she irritates me with another thing. She's chronically late for everything. And, uh . . . the only reason I can see for anyone being chronically late for everything is that they don't want to get there on time. I mean, you can be accidentally late just so often, but after that you start running out of reasons. . . . It's an appointment with the dentist, or church, or anything. And this irritates me, if nothing else.

COUNSELOR: There are a number of ways that you've mentioned that your mother irritates you. I'm not sure I know how you react to this annoyance.

> The counselor decided it was the anger he should have reflected.

PERSON: . . . Well, sometimes I end up arguing or something, but that gets me nowhere, really. Because, if anything, I just get in hotter water, which just gets me madder, which doesn't do any good any more. So I just kind of contain it and sort of simmer inside, or boil probably. Well, that's about the two choices I got, I guess. (With a tone of futility)

COUNSELOR: Seems like: "There isn't much else I can do about it."

PERSON: Yeah! (With a note of surprise, as if she were recognizing something for the first time) And, in a way, it's something I . . . I don't know what to do with. I . . . really want to try, and I'd like to just clear up everything. And sometimes, you know, I'll talk to her and try and clear things up, and she'll be halfway reasonable about it, or she seems like she is. And then the same thing happens again, and she . . . I don't know, she gets my brother pretty mad too. But he's not around like I am. Somehow, it seems like if there's any arguing, I get in on it. Or at least I'm the one who gets most of it. Somehow it seems like everybody else . . . kind of just takes it, and I'm the one who somehow has to express my anger.

The last comment led eventually, after some confrontation by the counselor (reported in the next chapter), to a recognition of her share of the responsibility for the constant friction with her mother. It turned out that each was trying to remake the other, a not uncommon phenomenon in this kind of situation.

Our last excerpt in this section was chosen to show how the counselor might respond to a nonverbal cue. It also raises the question of how he would deal with a moral issue concerning which it would be very easy to get directive or judgmental.

This is another college student, a young man about twenty. During the course of the session he had referred to on-campus drinking several times. Each time he shot the counselor a quick glance (the nonverbal cue) to see his reaction.

COUNSELOR: I wonder if you're aware that every time you tell me about breaking a school rule you look at me to see if I haven't gone "official" on you.

PERSON: Yeah. I know. But this *next* is pretty serious. I'm . . . I'm tellin' you just exactly . . . I'm copyin' . . . I copied a term paper for psychology, man!

COUNSELOR: Today you really are leveling . . . all the way.

PERSON: Yeah.

COUNSELOR: There isn't going to be much left when you get done.

PERSON: I . . . I . . . I sat down . . . I got it at a kid's room. He don't even know I have it, see. I'm . . . I'll be damned if I'm going to ask him if I can have it. But he's a pretty sharp kid, you know. And I figger, "Well, what the hell, you know, that term paper . . . they ain't gonna take photostatic copies of it and everybody read it, and everybody in the department couldn't read it. They'd be thumbin' through term papers clear to.last night. They wouldn't remember who wrote what anyhow."

COUNSELOR: But you're looking at me to see how I'm taking it.

PERSON: Yeah, I know it.

COUNSELOR: You're saying in effect: "Am I still going to like you? Am I still going to be concerned about helping you after I know all this stuff?"

PERSON: Well . . . yeah . . . I mean . . . when you find out really, you know. You'll be tellin' me what to do. Put the screws to me . . . "National Shaft-Your-Buddy Year" one more time. I don't know.

Sooner or later it might become necessary to confront this individual with the moral implications of his behavior, but at this stage of counseling the counselor felt that establishing a safe relationship was a much more critical issue. It was important for this person to see that he could disclose all of himself safely. As it turned out, he gave the counselor many other opportunities to confront him with himself morally.

5

Investigation, Interpretation, and Confrontation

The place to start an approach to counseling is with responding to the person's feelings and perceptions and reflecting these experiences back to him. It is the counseling method to be mastered before any other activity is undertaken. Unless the counselor can demonstrate to a distressed person that he can and will work to understand him, unless he can demonstrate that the counseling situation is a safe place in which to explore oneself, in short, unless a trusting relationship is established, there is no point to talking about any other type of counseling activity. There is no better way—in fact there probably is no other way—to establish trust than by reflecting the person's experiences back to him in an accepting, non-judgmental fashion. Such an approach also makes clearer than instructions can that the counselor expects the person to explore himself and that he believes the solutions to the person's problems must come primarily from within himself.

The place to begin a method of counseling is not necessarily the place to end. The predominant activity of the counselor need not be his only activity. In the early sessions of counseling close to a hundred percent of the counselor's responses ought to be in the reflecting-experience category. As counseling moves along, however, other kinds of responses become appropriate. We will consider (1) investigation, (2) interpretation, (3) confrontation, and (4) articulating the relationship.

Investigation

The Need for Information

The use of probing questions in counseling appears to be a natural and understandable counselor activity. After all, the counselor needs to know many things about a person in order to become acquainted with him—his age, occupation, education, family structure. He also needs to know the nature of his problems—when they began, how severe they are, how they affect his life, how he has been trying to cope with them. There are two tensions here. One is that the counselor has an honest need to know so that he can put the person and his problem into perspective; his own comfort as a counselor is involved. The other is that, by asking questions and inquiring into the other person's life, he runs the risk of threatening him and either impeding the counseling process or driving the person out of counseling altogether.

In some instances the pastor-counselor may be at an advantage over the secular counselor in this regard. The pastor often will already be in possession of considerable background information about the person he is counseling. There may not be as much tension to ask questions just to get a general orientation to the person seeking help.

Nevertheless, the hazard of asking even very simple questions can be pointed out. For example, the question "How many children do you have?" seems simple and innocuous. It is not, however, if the answer is, "Three children, one of whom is mentally retarded." The difficulty is that it is almost impossible to tell when a simple, innocuous question may turn into an emotionally loaded and threatening question. The general rule would seem to be that question asking should proceed with caution, if it is used at all. Furthermore the counselor who employs questions should be alert to cues that would indicate when sensitive points have been struck and when threat has been induced. When a threat has been induced, a reflection of this fact may be needed to save the day. For example, the counselor may find it desirable to reflect: "I embarrassed you with that question," or "You don't want to talk about that now," or "It's painful to think about that."

The counselor's felt need for more information may go in another direction. He may wish to know more about how the person experiences himself or his problem. This may be either to give himself a better understanding of the individual or because he believes it will help the person understand himself better and aid the process of problem resolution. To both points, we cannot repeat too often that probing in the form of direct questions can be hazardous. It can be threatening to ask, for example, "How did you feel when your mother said that?" or "What did you think of yourself after you'd done it?" The person may not be ready for such direct self-confrontation. Much, of course, will depend on the quality of the relationship that has developed between the person and the counselor. Such questions will have a different impact under different circumstances.

The Gentle Probe

There is a better way of getting information than asking direct questions. It might be called the *gentle probe*. The gentle probe is characterized by the tentative way it is phrased. It is couched in words that allow the individual maximum freedom in the way he responds. He can take the conversation in almost any direction his emotional needs dictate. He may even ignore the probe without bluntly refusing to deal with whatever issue the counselor wants to explore.

To be as helpful as possible we can again suggest some phrases that may help the counselor start a gentle probe. Expressions can be used like "I wonder how you feel about . . . " "I wonder what your thinking is when . . ." Sometimes it is not necessary to identify the subject of the probe, because that is evident from what has just been said. Then expressions like these may be useful: "Perhaps you have some feelings about that"; "I wonder if you could say a little more about how you see that"; "Perhaps you have some additional thoughts there."

The key words that make the counselor response a gentle probe rather than a direct question are words like *I wonder* and *perhaps*. These words connote that the counselor is not prejudging the question or pushing for a particular response by the person. He wonders, but he is leaving the issue up to the individual. If the person sidesteps or goes off on a different topic or deals with the question only superficially, the counselor follows where he leads. But often what follows is significant progress in the person's exploration of his experience.

An example follows from an interview with a college student who had a religious doubt problem. In the first part of the exchange he touches on his doubts regarding the Christian faith and his feelings of guilt about these doubts. He had previously explored in some detail his guilt feelings about living fraudulently but had never really gone into the nature of the doubts themselves. The counselor thought it might be valuable to give him a chance, by using a gentle probe, to examine the doubts. The excerpt shows how the person interprets the probe and how the counselor follows along.

PERSON: This really does bug me; I've got to do something about it. I've got to the point now where I have a lot of tension, and somehow there's got to be a cause for it. Somehow I've got to get rid of it. Now whether this talking will do it, or maybe it has to take something more drastic than this, I've gotten to the point now where I just don't want to put up with it anymore. It's not worth it. It's not worth it for any reason.

I used to think it was, but I don't any more. Because even if I did, let's say, force myself with all outward appearances to be a fine Christian, maybe *even somehow* be a churchgoer, well, I'd be miserable my whole life through. Because I just can't be happy when I feel so tense inside.

COUNSELOR: I wonder if you want to talk a little more about these doubts. (Probing)

PERSON: Well, see, in high school we got exposed in religion courses to a lot of different things. And I can see now, through all the years, a gradual change from the way it was taught in Sunday school to the way it seems to me now. I mean, when you always hear, like in Prof. X's class: "You gotta get *rid* of your Sunday school faith." And maybe, in a way, this is what I've been doing. Maybe I'm getting rid of it completely. (Nervous laughter.) But maybe it's only by struggling with it that you become stronger. I don't seem to see this in a lot of other people, though, that the attaining of a stronger faith is such a gruesome process. But what really was bad was my s-s-s-senior year ... uh ... I hung around with a boy who was a confirmed atheist.

COUNSELOR: Mmh hmn.

PERSON: And he really shook me up, 'cause I guess this was the first time I'd ever really known somebody that really didn't believe it. I mean, here was a guy that, I mean, he just couldn't accept what his parents had told him. Of course, we talked about it much, and it really bothered me. 'Cause he told me, he says: "Now I don't think you're a Christian at all." And I would try like heck to show him that I was. Somehow deep down I felt guilty, and I worried he was right.

COUNSELOR: This just sort of shook you at the roots somehow. (Back to reflecting)

PERSON: Sure did! 'Cause it seemed like he could see into me, whereas other people couldn't. I guess maybe I've been trying to deny it ever since.

Interpretation

The use of interpretation occupies a significant place in psychoanalytic therapy. It refers essentially to explaining to the person the meaning of his thoughts, feelings, or actions or the meaning of his past experiences and their effect in his life. It may also take the form of interpreting to the person the meaning of other people's behavior or giving him a more objective view of the world. This explaining, when properly used, provides more than intellectual knowledge, however. It produces an "insight" reaction with appropriate emotion and an inner sense of affirmation. Adequate interpretation depends on the counselor really knowing the correct explanations of a person's experiences and timing the giving of this information correctly. Correct knowledge and timing can only be achieved after the therapist has had long acquaintance with the person. Typical psychoanalytic interpretations might be telling the person that he really loves *and* hates his mother when he thought he only loved (or hated) her; or showing a person that his mistrust of people is the result of bad experiences with specific people in childhood. The hazards of interpretations are that they may be wrong, that they may be premature, that they may be unusable by the person, that they might frighten or repel the person.

There may be occasions when the pastor-counselor believes that interpretation is necessary. Finally, as we have said, the pastor has to work out his own approach to counseling. Some further discussion of this type of response follows therefore.

Interpretation is not the same as giving information. Many times in counseling it becomes evident that a person is simply in need of more information. For example, he wants to know whether he has the ability to accomplish a certain educational goal; he wants to know where he can get a job; he wants to know whether he really has a serious emotional problem. Counselors vary in their attitude toward supplying information. Some feel that it is one of their primary services as a counselor. However, counselors who take the general point of view espoused in this book tend to feel the opposite. They are willing to help the individual explore where he can get the information he wants; they are willing to help him explore its meaning for him when he gets it; but they will not put themselves in the position of handing out information like a parent or teacher. This underscores the basic question of what kind of stance the counselor will take in his work. Is he someone who tells what the answers are? Or is the counselor someone who helps another person find answers?

Requests for information are likely to come up in pastoral counseling in the form of religious questions and asking what the pastor thinks the person should do or think. Such questions are probably best dealt with by reflecting the person's desire to know rather than by giving out answers. If he follows such a strategy, however, the pastor-counselor should be ready to deal with the person's impatience, even anger, over the fact that he won't give answers. Nothing can do more, however, to demonstrate that the counselor believes the person is capable of solving his own problems and that the counselor can accept the person's feelings.

Interpretation is not a counseling activity that is totally different from what we have talked about so far. Actually, interpretation and reflecting experiences turn out to be on the same scale but at opposite ends. The scale involves the varying degrees to which a person is able to verbalize his personal experiences and their psychological meaning. At one end is what the person can put into words and express easily. At the other end is what lies outside of consciousness; this material the person cannot put into words or grasp the significance of. Reflecting experience and interpretation correspond to the opposite ends of the same continuum.

Reflecting experience consists of putting into words in a clearer and somewhat different way what is at or very near the surface of consciousness. It is not merely parroting the content of what the person says. It is a matter of distilling the essence of the feelings or perceptions and putting them into a few words so the person can see and experience them in a new way.

Interpretation is at the other end. It is putting into words something that is true and important concerning the person and is known to the counselor but is beyond what the person is able to understand by himself. For example, when a person has been talking about the fact that his wife left him, that he knows it is largely his own fault, and that he feels badly that he treated her as he did, it is not much of a leap beyond what the person is expressing for the counselor to *reflect* this and say: "You feel pretty responsible for what happened." But for the counselor to say, even on the basis of good evidence, "You drove your wife away because you can't tolerate becoming emotionally dependent upon another person," is an interpretation. The latter, no matter how correct it is, goes far beyond the "given" of what the person is expressing. Interpretation is probably best left largely in the hands of those highly skilled psychotherapists who do depth exploration of personality.

One difficulty in pastoral counseling is that offering interpretations is a very tempting business. The pastor by much past experience and training is geared to giving explanations and to offering people correct interpretations of life (just as he is prone to offer advice). He may be tempted to tell the person things like "You need more faith," "You should be more regular in your spiritual devotions," "You have hate in your heart," "You owe your husband his conjugal rights," "Youth should obey their parents." No matter how correct such interpretations may be, they are a hazard in counseling.

Gentle Interpretation

There are times when it is appropriate to go beyond the "immediately given" in what a person is expressing. That is, it is appropriate to offer something more than a mere reflection of what the person has been saying. As might be guessed, this should come relatively late in counseling, after a strong, trusting relationship is in existence. Furthermore, just as there is a difference between harsh probing and gentle probing, there can also be differences in interpretation.

One can distinguish between *dogmatic* interpretation and *gentle* interpretation. Dogmatic interpretation is an explanation offered as an incontrovertible fact. It implies that there must be something wrong with the person if he does not accept it. Gentle interpretation is offered as a hypothesis, something the counselor believes may be true, but he is not going to force it down the person's throat; it is something for the person to think about, not to accept blindly on authority. Such interpretations also do not go very far beyond what the person has been saying. They certainly do not involve either little lectures on how to think or wild "Freudian" explanations.

There is one kind of interpretation that particularly commends itself. This is the interpretation that calls a person's attention to the *ambivalences* within himself. In a sense, all psychological problems revolve around conflicts or ambivalences. The person feels two ways about something, and the feelings are incompatible; or he is pulled in two directions, but he cannot go both ways; or he wants two things, but he can't have his cake and eat it. To call attention to such ambivalence is a type of interpretation that does not go much beyond the usual response to feelings or perceptions, but it can get at conflicts of which the person has little or no awareness. Thus, for example, it is pointed out to him that he both likes and dislikes something. He finds someone both attractive and repulsive. He is both angry and pleased about something. He is afraid to take a certain action, yet he wants to do so badly. He is sad and remorseful over something, but at the same time he feels a certain pleasure about it. The possibilities are many and varied, of course. Only one further word of caution is needed. The counselor ought to be pretty sure he is on good ground before he offers such an interpretation. And he must be ready to acknowledge that his idea does not fit the person's experience if the person denies or rejects the suggestion.

Gentle interpretations can be broached with the same kinds of expressions that are used to launch a gentle probe: "I wonder if . . . ." "Perhaps you . . . ." These words connote the tentative, exploratory, nondogmatic quality of the counselor's intent. If the interpretation is a timely one, it will be picked up and explored further by the person. If the interpretation is untimely (even though it may be essentially correct), it will be ignored or denied. In the latter case, the counselor may want to respond to that. He may say something like "It doesn't seem that way to you," or "I misunderstood there." Sometimes such a reflection or admission by the counselor will bring about a surprising result. The person himself will then backtrack and admit that maybe what the counselor said is something to think about. In that way he is helped to start exploring the matter.

Here is an example of interpretation of ambivalence. This is the student with the vocational-choice problem again.

PERSON: But I mean . . . does a pastor really like, I mean, does he, I mean is he really happy about going to ladies guild and things like that?

COUNSELOR: You're saying: "It's hard to imagine pastors who like such things." (Reflecting)

PERSON: I mean, I just wondered. I know they do. I know they do this; I know they do that; but I mean, how much of it is a sense of duty? How much of anything is from a sense of duty? It seems to me duty's there somewhere, in just about everything you do.

COUNSELOR: So you see these two sides. Every job has its unpleasant obligations and its attractions.

> The interpretation goes beyond the "given" in that he has not really dealt with the attractions various jobs might have for him, although it is implicit in his previous comments.

PERSON: Right! But I do think there are some jobs I could do that would have more personal appeal to me as an individual than others. I don't want to be an engineer. I just couldn't stand it.

COUNSELOR: That would be confining, too, in some ways. (Reflecting)

PERSON: Yeah! It would be confining in that I'd be doing stuff I don't want to do. If that makes any sense. I just don't like to sit there and work out problems. I mean, I like . . . to me, freedom, in a sense, is freedom with people. People that I can . . . can really express my feelings and emotions about things with. (This was a new, more positive idea for him to express.)

In the next interview excerpt we are back to the woman who had problems with her mother. This session started with discussion of the idea that she expects other people to be hypercritical of her. Later in the interview she returned to talking about her mother. At that point the counselor thought it might be good to try to bridge the gap between her feelings about other people and her relations with her mother. As the excerpt shows, first she rejected the idea by agreeing with the counselor in a kind of hollow, unconvinced tone. Then when he backtracked, she started to explore further.

PERSON: I wish in a way, you know, that she'd do something about realizing what her problems are. I mean, she thinks it's everybody else with problems, and she has none. But . . . I really don't know what to do, or if anything could be done really until . . . she kind of decides that she wants to do something about it.

COUNSELOR: I wonder if you see any connection between all this, these relations between you and your mother, that is, and the idea that you started with today that you're supersensitive about whether other people notice your mistakes and remember them.

PERSON: . . . Maybe I could be. . . . Maybe I'm just sorta taking mother's reaction and transferring it to other people because I'm kind of used to this kind of thing. (Very hesitantly)

COUNSELOR: That doesn't altogether convince you, does it? (Backtracking)

PERSON: Well, in a way it does, because I mean . . . . Well it does partially *yes* and partially *no*. I can see how I could've gotten this kind of idea ingrained that I'll get a negative reaction . . . from the many experiences with her.

COUNSELOR: Sort of like you expect from everybody else the kind of reactions you get from her.

PERSON: . . . Well, what do you do then about, well, when you face other people who probably really aren't very critical? How do you stop transferring the idea that you will get a hostile reaction?

COUNSELOR: That's an issue that I think we're going to have to give some attention. I see our time is about up. Perhaps it's something you could reflect on between now and next time. (Continuing to gently press the issue)

PERSON: . . . It's going to be a kind of a different sort of thought . . . (Rising to go)

Confrontation

The counseling procedure called *confrontation* involves, as we have seen, confronting the person with some aspect of himself or his behavior. It is a recognized counselor activity in secular counseling, although it is not one that is generally stressed in textbooks or the professional literature.

Confrontation lends itself especially well to the counseling work of the pastor. It provides a therapeutically useful way to deal with the inner tension that may be generated within the pastor by his religious and moral commitments. As we noted, this is likely to involve moral issues, religious commitment, or the overall outcome of counseling.

When these kinds of issues come up in counseling, the bulk of the pastor's responses must continue to be those of reflecting experience. The pastor has to stay "in character." Thus, for example, he will continue to reflect that, as John sees it, there is no way out but divorce; that Mary Jane's angry attacks on her sister seem justified to her; that Paul's masturbation problem causes him great distress; that Mrs. Smith is "through" with the church. The pastor will not argue, persuade, console, or threaten. Instead he will help the person verbalize and examine his thoughts, feelings, and actions.

But there are limits to the usefulness of responding to experiences. The limit may be set by two factors. One factor is the pastor's own inner tension. The other factor may be an honest counselor judgment that it is important for the person to face himself in some area. That is, the pastor may feel that he could go on responding to experience but it is not to the person's best interests to do so. There are occasions in counseling where it is important for a person to face reality, or himself, or the implications of his behavior or intended behavior.

Confrontation can, of course, be inappropriate. Its effective use depends on a deep sense of trust. The person has to feel that the counselor really cares about him and that the counselor's words are meant to help, not to hurt. When that condition is met, it can be appropriate to confront an individual with some aspect of himself. He may be confronted, for example, with the fact that what he is contemplating is illegal, or endangers his life, or will be seriously detrimental to someone else. He may be confronted with clear teaching from God's Word that stands in opposition to his own intentions or actions. He may be confronted with a contradiction within himself, for example, that he thinks he is a good Christian but he is also seriously immoral in some way.

Gentle Confrontation

It is important to recognize that confrontation is carried out with the same attitude of willingness to let the person be himself and finally make his own decisions that characterizes all good counseling. Nothing is to be gained by getting emotional or manipulative. In confrontation the person's attention is drawn to the nature or implications of what he is saying, but he is allowed to take it from there. And that means literally that he really does determine the final outcome — even if it is not the choice the pastor would make for himself. For the counselor to hold a different point of view and yet honor the person's right to make his own decision is the mark of a truly capable counselor and a truly understanding human being. Nothing less is satisfactory for pastoral counseling.

Our first example of confrontation is from a counseling session with the young woman who had trouble getting along with her mother.

PERSON: Uh . . . well, once she was riding with me, and she was reading the newspaper in the car, and she was sitting in the front seat. Well, I don't particularly care to have somebody reading and blocking the view out the one side of the car when I'm driving. But I guess I could have passed it by. But . . . I asked her to put the newspaper away, and I knew this would probably irritate her. Well, I knew it *would* irritate her. Because I knew she wouldn't want to do it. And . . . I sort of ended up forcing my way. . . . This got her pretty mad. Somehow we always seem to be at odds. Sometimes I'll just take an opposite side, not because this side particularly appeals to me, but because she took the other side. I react and take the other side.

COUNSELOR: I wonder how you feel about yourself. I mean, the way you antagonize her. (Confrontation with her behavior)

PERSON: Well, I feel guilty about it in a way. I don't feel like I really should be irritating her. And I don't really feel like I should be angry about it after. There's something, you know, with your mother. You're not supposed to do this. And this plays into the business about . . . you know, when other people say, "You're a good daughter." Makes me feel guilty then too.

COUNSELOR: If other people admire you, you say to yourself: "But if you knew how I treat my mother!" (Reflecting but also continuing the confrontation)

PERSON: I really don't know why I do it unless it's that I feel somehow that she doesn't love me or something and . . . and . . . I don't think that's *exactly* it. But somehow, it seems like, if she loved me, she'd sort of take me the way I am, instead of this: "At home I treat you one way, and in front of other people I treat you another way." And somehow it seems like, if she loved me, she'd treat me fair, or something like this. . . . If I did something right, I'd get a little recognition, "Throw the dog a bone," or something.

Our second excerpt involves a much more vigorous kind of confrontation. This time we are dealing with a self-made businessman, a church elder who came for counseling because of dissatisfaction with his marriage. The wife was seen separately. Throughout most of his counseling sessions the husband had complained about his wife — her lack of interest in his work, her unwillingness to accompany him on out-of-town trips and to cocktail parties, which, as he saw it, were a necessary part of his business life, her preoccupation with their two children and disregard of his emotional needs. The only positive things he had to say about her were that she was a good housekeeper and a good church worker. In the previous session, he had for the first time gone into his complaints about her sexual unresponsiveness. Throughout all this time, although he occasionally made self-critical comments, the tone of his conversation implied that all the faults rested with her. The counselor felt the time had come to confront him with himself.

PERSON: (Ending a rather long passage of complaint) So, you see, I don't get much return for all my trouble. Seems like she could think about me a little more. If I weren't a church man and such, I think I might chuck the whole business . . . at least get a separation.

COUNSELOR: You feel justified in thinking you're getting a poor deal. But, you know, you've gone on and on about your wife's faults. I wonder where you fit in. I mean, I wonder what *you* do or what you *don't* do to make the marriage a success or failure.

PERSON: Well, I work pretty damn hard. Excuse my French, but I've worked hard to build up that business. Now I'm not saying she ain't a good wife in some ways. But I'm fed up with always gettin' "No" to everything I want. Just when we are gettin' to the place where we can do a few things, she doesn't want to do anything.

COUNSELOR: But I was wondering about your part in the dissatisfaction you feel. (Pressing the confrontation)

PERSON: Uh. . . . What d' ya mean? I don't know what you mean.

COUNSELOR: Well, I wonder what you think I might be getting at.

PERSON: You're sayin' maybe it's part my fault. I already told you that. I ain't claimin' to be no saint. Now if she'd be . . . more —

COUNSELOR: (Interrupting) John, I wonder if you're not ducking the issue.

From this point on, the counseling took a noticeably different turn. Gradually at first, and with some additional pressing by the counselor in later sessions, John began to spend more time examining himself and less time reciting his wife's faults. The counselor believes that had a blunt confrontation been made early in counseling, the result would have been quite disastrous. John would have paid lip service to his own involvement, but he probably would have terminated counseling soon thereafter. If he had been allowed to go on reciting his complaints, it is uncertain whether he would ever have looked at himself clearly. As it turned out, he did go on, and there was a lot more involved than merely the wife's uncooperativeness and the husband's complaints. Among other factors, there had been sexual infidelity on the husband's part, which was known by the wife but had never been openly faced by the couple. This had caused the wife to withdraw emotionally from the relationship even though she did not want to get a divorce.

Articulating the Relationship

There is still another counselor activity we wish to examine. It too involves a more interventionist role for the counselor than just reflecting feelings and perceptions. Like interpretation, it may go beyond what the person has actually expressed. Or, like confrontation, it may bring the person face to face with something he has been avoiding. For lack of a better term, we will call it *articulating the relationship* between the counselor and the individual.

First, a few background comments. There are many approaches to counseling and psychotherapy—client-centered, psychoanalytic, rational-persuasive, existential, and behavioristic. An interesting but rather disconcerting fact is that all these approaches seem to work to some extent. None of them seems to be so universally successful that one can say, "This is the method and theory to choose." It may very well be that the reason any of them work is largely independent of their theory and technique. That is, they may work for some other reason, and the different theories and methods are less important than we think. The possibility exists that this other "something," this "vital ingredient," that cuts across all forms of therapy is the quality of the *relationship* that develops between the person and the therapist.

If a strong sense of trust develops, and if the relationship is open and honest for both parties, the person will experience himself more fully and move in the direction of solving his problems regardless of the method the counselor is using. If it is not that kind of relationship, counseling will probably fail. It may be this, for example, that allows the client in client-centered therapy to go on exploring himself and become more open to his own experience. The same quality may allow the analysand to accept the psychoanalyst's interpretations of his Oedipus complex. At any rate, whether or not *relationship* is the whole story, it certainly is a vital ingredient in all or most forms of treatment.

Counselor-Counselee Reactions

Untrained counselors tend to shy away from coming to grips with the feelings and thoughts they have about their counselees and the feelings and thoughts they suspect the person has toward them and toward counseling. For example, the counselor is reluctant to deal with the possibility that the person is annoyed with him or that the person is developing sexual feelings toward him. He would be even more reluctant to verbalize that he has similar feelings and thoughts about the person or about the way counseling is going. Somehow, counseling (especially the counselor) is supposed to be void of such personal reactions. Thoughts about the past, feelings about other people, and personal problems are all fair subjects for talk. Feelings and thoughts about each other are to be avoided. The reason is that such thoughts are too threatening to both parties.

But if such reactions exist, they constitute a hidden factor that has an important bearing on the process of counseling. If the feelings or thoughts are negative and they are not given expression, they will sabotage the endeavor. If they are positive and they must be kept under cover, they will keep the person from becoming as free and open and spontaneous a human being as he can become. Either outcome is regrettable.

Articulating the relationship means putting into words, saying aloud, what the counselor believes the person may be experiencing or what he himself is experiencing about the relationship between them. Often this is no more than articulating what the person has been expressing. Then it is a reflection of experience. For example, the counselor may say something like, "You're afraid that I'll think you're an awful person," or "You're discouraged about the way counseling is going" (if these are the things the person has been saying). But the counselor may go beyond what the person has expressed and use a gentle probe or an interpretation — "I wonder if you aren't concerned about how I feel about you" (probe); or "It seems to me you must be pretty angry with me" (interpretation). The counselor must, of course, have some cues on which to base his response.

The counselor may choose to confront the individual with some aspect of the relationship. "You keep saying that I'm not helping you because I won't tell you what to do. I wonder why you keep coming back, if this is not helping"; or "You've hinted several times that you have some thoughts about my competence as a pastor. I wonder if you could bring them out in the open."

Reactions of the Person

Some of the common thoughts and feelings that individuals develop toward counselors and counseling are these:

In the early stages the person is likely to be concerned with what the counselor thinks of him. He may expect disapproval. He may debate whether or not he really has a significant problem (which is often only a symptom of his reluctance to dig deeper). He may have doubts about the competence of the counselor. He may have fears that nothing can help him. He may be concerned about how to relate to the pastor-counselor outside of counseling. Articulating these kinds of concerns is appropriate right from the beginning. In fact, whether or not a true counseling relationship ever develops may depend on whether the counselor is able to pick up subtle cues about such reactions and get them out in the open.

In later stages the counselor should be ready to respond to other possibilities. The person may worry about whether the counselor really likes him or is only concerned about him professionally. Sometimes the individual develops intense feelings of love, hate, or anger toward the counselor, which must be articulated. Sometimes the person wants to be taken care of like a child or treated with kid gloves, or he wants to have a part in the counselor's personal life. Such feelings of love, anger, dependency, and personal interest are examples of *transference*. Transference reactions tend to be kept to a minimum in the kind of counseling we have described, but when cues for them come up, they should be dealt with.

Finally, toward the close of counseling, the person may have feelings about ending the counseling relationship that have to be articulated. These may include reluctance to give up a safe, comfortable relationship, fear of going it alone, and concern about how to relate to the counselor in the future.

Reactions of the Counselor

How to deal with the counselor's thoughts and feelings is somewhat more problematic. The pastor is certain to have reactions. There will be things about the person he likes and dislikes. He too will have thoughts about his own competence and whether or not counseling is helping the person. He will find himself getting bored or annoyed or overly concerned about the person he is trying to help. He may have thoughts of a sexual nature or dreams about him or her. He may experience impulses to overprotect, console, warn, or scold the person.

What shall he do with such reactions? The attitude that guides the counselor in dealing with tensions arising from his commitments as a pastor can guide him here also. He does not blurt out these reactions at the first sign of their appearance. But when they persist and when they cause significant tension in him, then they too must be articulated. For if they are not brought out in the open, they will make their appearance in devious ways and jeopardize the counseling relationship. When they are brought into the open, they can be dealt with just like any other reaction.

When these feelings and thoughts whelm up, the pastor may very well make comments like, "You know I find myself getting annoyed with you lately. I wonder why"; or "I guess I'm concerned about what you are going to do. I wish you wouldn't, but the decision is yours"; or "I find myself wanting to comfort you and say, 'Don't worry.' But I don't think that would be helpful to you"; or "I'm concerned too about the way things are going. It bothers me that I'm not being more helpful." He might even find it necessary to say something like, "I find you sexually provocative, and I find myself being disturbed by it."

Feelings and thoughts of this sort are not unnatural. But if the pastor finds himself developing intense feelings about the counseling relationship with frequency, he should seriously *confront himself.* Perhaps he cannot work with this person and should refer him or her elsewhere. Perhaps he should talk it over with another pastor or a mental health professional. Perhaps he should work it out in his own therapy.

Or perhaps he should decide to stay away from counseling altogether and stick to pastoral care.

Two excerpts from counseling sessions follow. In the first, the counselor is working with a college student who was in the last stages of flunking out of school, not because he wasn't bright enough but because he rarely studied. In the previous session the counselor had been probing to get him to explore his pattern of studying, possibly harder than good counseling would allow. In this context the topic of the student's being required by his academic advisor to make out a daily study schedule and turn it in had arisen. The advisor wrote comments of commendation or disapproval on these forms. The counselor had probed on this point also. In the session from which the excerpt is taken, the student expressed considerable anger at the humiliation of having to turn in these daily reports. The counselor surmised from various cues that this annoyance might extend to himself also because he had probed so hard in this area. He felt he ought to try to get this out in the open if it existed.

COUNSELOR: You had a lot of feelings about those study schedules.

PERSON: I hated that. Oh, I hated to make out those cards. I really did! Sometimes I felt good. Sometimes I hated it. But I thought it was, you know, kinda ridiculous. What's "good" mean, or what's "excellent" mean? Well, I mean, is that supposed to mean somethin' to me? I even hate to talk about it.

COUNSELOR: I wonder if you weren't pretty angry with me too for pushing you to talk about it. (Articulating the possible relationship)

PERSON: Yeah. I guess I thought you was laughin' about it. You know: "Ha, ha . . . that poor slob here. Look what he's doin'." Uh, uh! No sir! I wanted . . . I . . .

I, you know, no hard feelings, I hope, but that really ticks me off.

COUNSELOR: Mmh hmm.

PERSON: After our session was over and I went back to my room, I cried. I laid down on the bed, and I thought to myself: "Why in the hell don't they just leave me alone, and I'll come out of it. I'll get the attitude, and I'll *do* it [study]. They don't have to say nothin' to me. Why don't they just mind their own business? Why do they have to care?" I don't . . . I don't know why it is that way with me that I have to . . . I have to rebel every time somebody reprimands me for something. I do it that much more.

The person then went on to explore further his feelings about being nagged to do what he ought to do. As might be expected, these feelings had a long history. The excerpt is also a good example of how much feeling can be generated in a person by what to someone else may seem like a rather innocuous and well-intentioned effort (making out a daily report).

The second excerpt is from a session with the student quoted at the end of the last chapter, the one who talked about drinking on campus and stealing a psychology paper to copy. This time he had been talking about sexual behavior. The counselor assumed that the student might have some feelings about how he reacted to this information.

COUNSELOR: There's kind of a big issue here about how I feel about you . . . whether I can like you if I know all this stuff. (Focusing on the feelings they may have about each other)

PERSON: . . . Well, probably . . . I don't know . . . I just . . . I know I never told anybody that. I swore up and

down I'd never tell anybody. I'd never tell anybody about . . . about these things.

COUNSELOR: I wonder how you feel now that they're out.
(Continuing with a gentle probe)

PERSON: Well . . . like a lot of other things that I've said to
to people that I thought I'd never tell. I just
wonder. You know, I mean, Emerson says that a
friend is somebody that whom when I'm with
I can think out loud. I wrote a paper on that once.
My junior year in high school. I never found anybody like that in my life. Somewhere, sometime,
somehow, it always comes out. And for somebody
shrewd enough to put two and two together, they
can always come up four. And I don't know . . .
I . . . if it comes out, it comes out. I don't care.
. . . (Softly) I care, but . . . you know . . . I'll overcome it, somehow.

COUNSELOR: You say, even if I let you down, you'll get by.
That says, in effect, that maybe in some way you
expect that probably I will.

PERSON: Well, maybe it's just that I've never known anybody that didn't. . . . But I don't know. The way
I figure it, you've got to be prepared for the worst.
. . . I . . . (Continues to explore his rather cynical
theories about people)

6

Some Practical Issues
and Counseling Ethics

There are additional considerations about counseling not covered in the previous chapters that are worthy of our attention. For convenience we will consider them under five headings: Decisions Prior to Counseling, Opening Phases of Counseling, Counseling Proper, Ending Issues, and Counseling Ethics.

Decisions Prior to Counseling

There are a number of "practical" decisions the counselor needs to make before he ever begins a counseling relationship.

How Much Counseling?

Probably the first such decision he should make is just how much counseling he is in a position to do. Counseling is a time-consuming business. It usually involves 1 or 2 hours a week for each person being counseled, although in some instances half-hour sessions are suitable. Except for a handful of pastors who are called specifically to perform a counseling ministry, it is hard to see how the average pastor is in a position to see more than a few persons a week for pastoral counseling.

The pastor must be mindful of the limits of his own strength and the proper stewardship of his time over against *all* the demands of the present-day ministry. Just as important, he must consider his obligations to the people to whom he offers counseling. If a pastor spreads himself too thin, if he establishes more counseling contacts than he can comfortably handle, he may damage the very people he wishes to help. Frequent breaking of appointments at the last minute can be extremely threatening to a troubled person. Counseling requires a comfortable, relaxed atmosphere. If the pastor sits with one eye on the clock because he has to be downtown in 20 minutes or he wishes he were free to do something else, this will be sensed by the person, and it will be disruptive of counseling.

There is no place in pastoral counseling for the counselor who keeps adding case after case to his counseling load until he develops the attitude of an overburdened martyr. Whether or not there is a place for such unlimited willingness to be helpful in pastoral *care* may be debatable — one runs across pastors who are literally driving themselves to an early grave — but for pastoral counseling the answer is clear. The pastor should decide how many hours a week he can devote to counseling and what days and hours are comfortable for him, and he should stick to them.

With Whom?

A second important decision the pastor has to make is to whom he will actually offer counseling. Many people do not have a clear conception of counseling as a sustained, regular series of consultations. This is gradually changing with the increasing familiarity of the public with psychotherapy, and it will change further once a pastor becomes known as a counselor, but most people who seek a pastor's help in their distress are thinking in terms of one or two consultations. Consequently, the pastor is usually in a position to *offer* counseling to a selected few individuals out of all the persons who come to him for help. The rest he can handle on the basis of pastoral care.

The decision to offer pastoral counseling involves two considerations: the nature and severity of the person's difficulty, and the "psychological readiness" of the pastor to deal with a particular person or problem on a counseling basis. The question of the nature and severity of the problem will be examined further in the next chapter, but briefly stated, the pastor's chief counseling activity is with persons with "normal" problems or with mild to moderate symptomatology.

The question of "psychological readiness" refers to whether the pastor feels comfortable with a particular kind of problem or person. The pastor may feel disqualified and not offer counseling for a number of reasons. For example: He is uncertain how severe the problem is, and he is unwilling to get involved in a problem that may lie beyond his competence. Or the problem for some reason is repulsive to him. He shrinks from a problem involving homosexuality or pederasty. Or he is reluctant because he has had other dealings with the individual that would make counseling uncomfortable for one or both of them. It may be that he has had a "run-in" with the person, or close social or family relationships are involved. In short, unless the pastor can enter counseling with a sense of reasonable confidence and comfort, he would do better to restrict his services to the individual to pastoral care.

When we talk here about offering pastoral counseling, we literally mean *offering*. That is, the pastor suggests (in a gentle probing manner) that perhaps the person would like to explore the problem that brought him to the pastor in a series of regular counseling sessions. In some instances the pastor may be somewhat more "interpretive" and suggest that he thinks it would be helpful to the person to enter such a relationship. The decision is, of course, left to the individual.

Records

A third practical question concerns the kind of record the pastor is going to keep of the counseling process and what use he will make of it. A professional counselor should keep some kind of carefully guarded record of his counseling contacts with each person. At the very least this should include the dates on which a person was seen, with notes on the general content of each session. Periodically the counselor should review these and put in writing an estimate of what is going on in counseling and what questions require his thought and attention. (Some counselors do this after every session.)

Some counselors take notes during counseling, but others, perhaps most, find that taking notes prevents them from responding fully to what the other person is expressing. Note-taking thus interferes with the counseling process. Tape-recording is an easy means of recording the content of sessions, but it requires eventual condensation and transcription to paper if the counseling record is to be reduced to manageable size and used.

Tape recordings are particularly useful for evaluation of what is really happening in counseling. They give the counselor a chance to hear things he may have been missing. They allow him to hear how he himself actually has been responding, which may be at variance with what he thought he was doing. Tape-recording is probably a *must* for the pastor who seriously wants to work out his own approach to counseling. A tape recorder can be threatening to the person being counseled, but most counselors simply make it a part of the counseling procedure and find that people soon take it for granted. If the person is threatened by it, this is dealt with just as any other issue that comes up during counseling, that is, by *reflecting* the concern and working it through.

Where?

A final question is where counseling will take place. Counseling requires a relatively small room (for a sense of privacy), with soft lighting and comfortable chairs. It must be absolutely free of distractions. This means literally disconnecting the

telephone or telling the secretary that there are to be no inter-
ruptions for anything short of an earthquake.

Opening Phases of Counseling

Exploratory Sessions

What does the pastor do when he has offered to begin
counseling and the person has expressed willingness or at
least interest? Obviously, the first step is to set the time and
place for the first meeting. Often it is desirable to structure
this as an exploratory session in which the person can see
if he wants to undertake this kind of program. In such an
exploratory session the counselor responds just as he would
in any counseling hour, but it gives the person a feeling of
control over the situation and makes it clear he can withdraw
if he wishes. Sometimes the exploration process takes more
than one session. It can also happen that the person decides
not to continue with counseling because he believes he can
handle his problem himself. The exploratory process was just
the "therapy" he needed.

Reactions to Starting Counseling

Most people who come to a pastor for help in distress are
ready to reveal at least part of what disturbs them. But a number of things can happen to this intention. By the time the
person gets to the first counseling session, he is no longer so
ready to talk. Perhaps the urgency of the problem has subsided somewhat. Perhaps anxiety about what he may reveal
has risen to block his thoughts. Or perhaps the person is not
ready yet to talk about the "real" problem, so he starts off
with a safer problem or a part of the real problem that isn't
too painful. It may happen that the person will "tell his problem," possibly in the first session or two, and then stop talking

and wait for advice. Or if he knows he is not going to be given answers, he may complain that there is nothing more to say in an unconscious attempt to maneuver the counselor into "taking charge."

Thus various combinations of "blocking," inability to get started, inability to keep talking, and the increase of symptoms like anxiety, sweating, and weepiness are likely to arise in the early stages of counseling. These are technically called *resistances,* and they jeopardize the relationship. Clearly the responses of the counselor are crucial. The most effective thing the counselor can do is to *reflect*—for example, that it is hard to get started, that the person feels empty of further ideas, that he feels weepy or apprehensive, or whatever he seems to be experiencing.

Two reactions that warrant special mention are *flight into health* and sudden *panic.* Sometimes shortly after counseling has begun, or even in the interval before it begins, the person experiences a rather dramatic sense of improvement in his situation. What was bothering him seems insignificant, and he feels much better. In fact life looks rosier than it has for a long time. This almost always represents a defensive reaction. It means that the person's anxiety is rising and that natural defensive processes are coming to his "rescue." Sometimes the person is even aware of what is so threatening. He knows he is going to have to talk about some aspect of himself he is ashamed of. The nearer he gets to revealing the dangerous topic the more threatening it becomes until suddenly, as if by magic, he feels much better. Usually the person will have no insight into what has happened.

The other reaction involves a "flight" into more severe symptomatology. At the start of counseling or just before, the person experiences a sudden increase in symptoms or a new set of symptoms that result in a panic or near-panic reaction. The person feels frightened for no apparent reason. His problem seems much more serious than it did before. He may become terrified that he is losing his mind. Since this occurred contiguous with the decision to start counseling, the person concludes that if he will now only withdraw from the counseling relationship, these terrible feelings will go away.

This flight toward panic usually represents only a defensive reaction, but for the pastor it involves the additional complication of having to decide whether the problem is one that is beyond his competence. There is a possibility that the increased anxiety may trip off more serious emotional reactions. The pastor has to make a professional judgment as to whether to continue the counseling relationship or refer the person elsewhere. Generally it is safe to continue as long as the person keeps complaining and talking about his increased distress. But if the person begins to show signs of severe disorder, referral should be made or professional consultation sought.

Keeping Talk Going

An important question is how the pastor can get the individual started, keep him talking, and cope with his emotional reactions to talking. Suppose the problem is one where the person comes for the first counseling hour and finds he cannot get started talking. Then it is appropriate for the pastor to respond something like this: "You find it hard to begin," or "You don't know how to get started." If the problem is one where the person has divulged the problem and then cannot think of anything more to say, the pastor may respond: "It seems like there's nothing more to say," or "You've run against a blank wall." If the person has said or given cues that he is afraid to go on, this should be reflected — "It frightens you when you talk about these things," or "It's hard to say out loud what you are thinking." If the person volunteers that the problem has practically disappeared, the counselor will respond to this—"You had a problem when we first talked, but now it doesn't seem so important," or "You don't see much need for going into this further." If the issue is one of increased symptomatology or panic, the counselor's response should pick this up—"Things have gotten worse since I saw you last," or "You're afraid, but you don't know why, and that's pretty upsetting." Such responses will usually help the person go on, and therein lies the hope of solution.

Structuring the Relationship

Sometime during the first counseling session it is desirable for the counselor to start to *structure the counseling relationship*. This is a way of saying he needs to convey to the person the ground rules under which they are operating. Different counselors handle this differently. Some simply begin responding in their usual manner. They allow the person to discover for himself that this relationship is different from most relationships and that the counselor is not going to take over, ask questions, give advice. Other counselors find it useful to explain how they operate, knowing full well that one explanation can't be fully assimilated by the person but believing that it gives a starting point.

The counselor might say something like this: "It's my understanding that there are some things that are bothering you . . . that you'd like help with . . . and that we're going to try to work on them together here. I find that I'm most comfortable in counseling if I explain to a person a little bit about how I work. I see my primary job here as trying to understand how you feel so I can help you understand yourself more fully. I'd like you to talk as freely as you can about what's bothering you; but I know that's not always easy. One thing you won't find me doing, at least not very much, is giving you advice or answers for your problems. My experience is that the best solutions for problems are the ones people work out for themselves. . . . I'd also like to explain that this is an entirely free situation. The hour is yours to talk about what seems most important to you. . . . I assume we'll keep meeting as long as you find it helpful. . . . Perhaps you'd like to start talking about what's bothering you, how you see things."

What the counselor hopes he is conveying is: (1) He wants to help, (2) he thinks the answers to the person's problems lie in the person, (3) the person is free to talk about whatever he wants to talk about, (4) the person has control over how long counseling will continue, and (5) the counselor expects the person to start telling about himself.

Structuring the situation is not something that can be done once and then forgotten. It is a continuing process, especially during the early stages of counseling. Only a certain amount of information and understanding can be conveyed to the person by words. The person must learn largely from the experience itself what counseling is like and what the counselor does and does not do. After the initial verbal structuring of the situation, structuring is continued by how the counselor responds.

Ending the Hour

Toward the end of the first session it is usually desirable to reconfirm whether the person wishes to continue the counseling relationship and, if so, to confirm the regular meeting time. The counselor might say something like this about 5 minutes before the end of the hour: "Well, I guess it's getting close to the time to stop for today. . . . I wonder if you wish to continue with counseling." If the reply is affirmative, the meeting time is agreed upon. If the reply is negative or shows ambivalence, an attempt is made to pick up this feeling—for example, "You won't be coming back again," or "You haven't found this very satisfactory." The exact response depends, of course, on the cues the person supplies. If pursuit of the person's reactions leads to a decision to return, the time of meetings is reconfirmed. If the person's negative reaction does not change, this is accepted and counseling ends. Usually some additional statement is made by the counselor that counseling will be available should the person find that he wants to return.

Sometimes a bit of awkwardness arises about how to end the hour. If the person does not terminate the session by indicating that he is ready to leave, the counselor ends the hour by simply saying something like, "Well, I guess our time is up for today," and rising. If both parties are to remain comfortable about counseling, it is important that the hour not be allowed to run on and on. It is also important that the counselor not take responsibility for always ending the session. If this occurs, it needs to be dealt with like any issue of concern in counseling.

Questions the Person Raises

It may happen during the early phases of counseling that the person asks direct questions about the counseling relationship or makes direct complaints about what the counselor does or does not do.

The person may ask: "When am I going to get some answers?" or "When are you going to start helping me?" At this point it is again critical that the counselor stay in character. He may, for example, respond: "I'm not doing what you'd like me to do," or "This doesn't seem to be helping much." If this response leads to annoyance, the counselor will reflect that also. The person may say something like, "Well, does everybody think this way, or is it just me? Oh, I know you won't answer my questions! You never do!" The counselor then will reflect the person's annoyance or dissatisfaction—for example, "You are irritated with me," or "You expected something else from counseling."

It must be remembered that the expression of anger may

involve something beside dissatisfaction with the counselor. It may be a way of testing the counselor to see if he really *is* accepting. Or it may be the person's first tentative step in the direction of releasing emotions, and the counselor's method may be only a convenient issue about which to vent some steam. If the counselor becomes defensive and starts explaining his method, or asks the person to have confidence in him, or gives in to the person's complaints, it can hinder the development of the counseling relationship.

It will sometimes happen that a person starting pastoral counseling will ask whether special fees are involved for this prolonged, time-consuming service. Or the person may wish to show appreciation by giving gifts to the pastor-counselor. The tradition of the ministry is, of course, not to accept gifts and fees for counseling services. The general principle of not accepting fees for pastoral counseling is a sound one. If nothing else, it eliminates any question of the pastor's monetary motives.

On the other hand, it is a recognized principle among mental health workers that it is frequently important for a person to pay for his counseling or psychotherapy. It makes the service more meaningful if it costs something, and it eliminates the feeling that one is the recipient of charity. The person can feel that he paid for the help he got and owes no one. Some agencies have a principle of charging a minimum fee per session, even if it is only a token amount. In some cases the pastor too may feel that paying a fee would be important for a particular person. It is valuable in these cases to set a counseling fee and let the person send the money to some worthy cause. This retains the values of paying for counseling without compromising the position of the pastor with respect to accepting fees.

Attempts to reward the pastor with gifts or favors can be dealt with by attempting to understand what the person feels inside and responding to it. It may lead to counselor responses like, "You want to show your appreciation for what's happening here," or "It bothers you to think you are taking so much of my time." It's a stickier problem if the counselor suspects he is being manipulated or his favor sought through gifts, but the relationship will have to be articulated.

Counseling Proper

One might think that this ought to be a long section. Actually there is not a great deal that can be said about what actually happens in counseling except in connection with particular people with specific problems. It is impossible to present procedures beyond those already indicated in previous chapters, so this section is limited to a few general topics.

Feelings

If the pastor does an adequate job of responding to a person's *feelings* in counseling, he will find this leads to still further release of inner experience and feeling. Emotions whelm up in the person that have gone unexpressed for a long time. Sometimes they will come out easily and spontaneously but often only after a hard struggle. To the person they seem dangerous, silly, embarrassing, childish, or revolting. Sometimes they are accompanied by a sense of relief, sometimes by anxiety. One of the jobs of the counselor is to use the cues the person provides in order to infer what is being held back or what is just below the surface and to help the person express it. Hence he must be sensitive to subtle cues—an idea that hints at underlying emotion, a tremor in the voice that suggests weepiness, a facial expression of disgust, the clench of a fist that conveys anger, the stiffness of posture that indicates tension.

The pastor can expect to see deep inner feelings come out in counseling. He will hear people describe *hostility*—anger that has long been bottled up, dislike for parents or spouse, annoyance with a friend, anger at social injustice or at the church. He will see *guilt* in its many forms—guilt over anger and hate; guilt associated with sex, theft, fraud, and jealousy; guilt that is real and guilt that is unwarranted. He will confront *shame* and *humiliation*. He will hear stories of *shyness* and *embarrassment*—people too shy to ask for help, too self-conscious to speak in public. He will see people weep and then be ashamed because "Grown-ups don't cry!" *Fear* and *anxiety* will come out—fear of what others are thinking, fear of death, fear of finding that one's worst fears are realized, anxiety that seems to have no basis.

The pastor will encounter many temptations to step out of his role of responding to the person's inner experience. But if the pastor sticks to his role, he will usually be rewarded eventually with positive reactions from the person. He will see the person begin to question whether his past feelings were appropriate. He will watch the person sort out the appropriate feelings from the distorted feelings. He will hear reports of things that are going well for the person, feelings that are pleasant. Most important, he will watch as the person learns to accept and live with his feelings.

Distortions

The pastor can assume that as the person talks he will also reveal *distortions in his thoughts and perceptions.* If these distortions are gross, so that the person reports hearing voices or seeing things, or if they are delusional and the person expresses ideas that can't possibly be true, the pastor will have to make a referral. But there is a wide range of distortions that are not indicative of gross pathology. There is the man who sees himself as incompetent, although the evidence is to the contrary. There is the young woman who fears she is not attractive enough to get a husband, the adolescent who thinks his sexual phantasies are as bad as if they were acted out. There are many people who can tell themselves they are forgiven by God, but they feel so guilty that they cannot accept and forgive themselves. The pastor will be amazed to discover how often what seems monstrous and completely unforgivable to another person seems trivial and easy for him to understand.

He will discover that events of the past are sometimes distorted out of all proportion to their original significance. One counselee literally shook with fright as he described what it had meant, as a youngster, to come home and tell his parents that his bicycle had been stolen. He audibly sighed with relief when this incident was out in the open. A woman slowly and painfully recalled her shame when she wet herself in the 3rd-grade classroom. A pastor who was being counseled saw himself as unfit for the ministry because he had a long-standing masturbation problem.

We believe that the pastor can best deal with these kinds of distortions by reflecting back to the person his experience. Sometimes the person will immediately see the distortion in his views. Sometimes the self-correction takes longer, and only gradually does the person come to question his previous ideas and perceptions. In the meantime the counselor attempts to see things through the person's eyes. He doesn't have to accept the person's perception of things as his own reality, but he can be expected to accept them as the person's reality and respond accordingly.

Sometimes counselees distort matters that are near and dear to the heart of the pastor. The person may say something like, "I know fourteen families that are going to transfer their membership to St. John's," or "Everyone says Pastor Plunk has the best sermons in this district," leaving the pastor to wonder where he rates. The pastor-counselor is cautioned not to take to heart the remarks heard in counseling. It is almost impossible to separate the distortions from the realities. He must remember that the reason the person is there is because he has serious problems with his perceptions of himself and his world. The pastor will pass the acid test of his ability to understand and accept if he can reflect back these perceptions without flinching or, if the tension and threat become too great, can bring his own feelings out in the open.

Silence

One of the things many counselors have to learn is to be comfortable with silence. The fact is that most people in our day do not tolerate silence well. (This is why many people must constantly have the radio playing or the television going.) In the counseling process silence can be a valuable tool. The counselor must learn to sit quietly and wait for the person to go on. At first silence of 40 or 50 seconds may seem like eternity. But as he gains confidence in himself and his counseling, the pastor will find that this silence can be very productive. Then silence lasting 2 or 3 minutes will not make him uncomfortable. Not only will the counselor learn to be comfortable with silence, but people in counseling often learn it also. It is not unusual to have a person say that for the first time he can be quiet and not be anxious. This is usually part of a growing realization by the person that he can be himself and that he does not have to be afraid of himself or his thoughts.

There are hazards in the use of silence, however. The chief hazard is that the person will be made too uncomfortable by silence and be driven away. The person feels he should talk, but nothing comes. The silence becomes unbearable. At these times the counselor needs to help the person by reflecting this fact—"It's hard to get started"; "You feel you can't say what you are thinking." Or the counselor may use a gentle probe that encourages the person to go on—"I'm not sure I understand how you feel about—" (referring to something the person said previously).

Another hazard in the use of silence is that it can become a hostile act on the part of the counselor. The counselor puts the person on the spot and makes him feel uncomfortable by not helping to keep the conversation going. Or silence is used to pry into matters that the person is not yet ready to explore. Clearly such uses of silence are to be avoided. In actual practice the use of silence has to be based on the cues in the situation.

Working Through, Catharsis, Insight

As the counseling process proceeds, the counselor is likely to encounter three phenomena: *working through, catharsis,* and *insight.* In *working through,* the person goes over the same material again and again. He talks repeatedly, for example, about what is bothering him in his marriage, always, of course, in slightly different ways and usually adding to and clarifying his feelings and perceptions. To some extent this reflects his struggle to understand the problem. It can also reflect a need to go over the situation again and again to desensitize it or to be sure he really understands. Sometimes beginning counselors think that such repetition means counseling has bogged down and that the person is getting nowhere. Actually what is happening is that the person chips away at his problems little by little, gradually moving deeper into them. What may seem insignificant and repetitious to the counselor is likely to be vital to the person in his struggle for self-understanding.

A second phenomenon the pastor will encounter is *catharsis.* Catharsis refers to the sense of relief that accompanies unburdening one's self. The person divulges feelings, thoughts, or behavior that he has long kept hidden, often with a great deal of emotion. When he does let them out, he may feel a sense of well-being bordering on pure joy. The same effect is commonly seen in private confession. Among professional counselors it is generally recognized that catharsis alone is not adequate for most emotional problems. The person also needs to explore the origin of his guilt and the reasons why he has kept the matter hidden, and to work it through until it has lost its capacity to cause distress.

A third phenomenon the pastor will encounter is that the person really does come to understand himself better. Sometimes this occurs rather suddenly and with emotion. The person may actually exclaim: "Why, I never realized that before!" or "I certainly never expected to find myself—[feeling, thinking, or acting in a certain way]." At other times the development of self-understanding is much more gradual and is seen by the person more as a growing awareness of self. Gradual or sudden, this is referred to as the development of *insight.*

Insight is not limited to *self*-understanding. The person may also develop insight into the behavior and feelings of others and into the meaning of past events in his life. For example, a woman came to understand for the first time how her husband must feel when she berated him in public. (Then she had to work through her guilt about that.) Another person discovered why he always felt uneasy in the presence of ministers. As a child his parents had been in constant marital strife, and the minister was frequently called in to make peace. Unconsciously he had come to associate ministers with emotional turmoil.

Ending Issues
How Long?

How long counseling lasts depends on the nature of the person and his problems. In simple problems counseling may be only a matter of a few sessions, perhaps a half dozen. In more difficult problems counseling is likely to last at least 30 or 40 sessions, and sometimes counseling will run to a hundred sessions or more. Most pastors will probably find one session a week the most convenient arrangement, but the pastor may wish to experiment with sessions every 2 weeks and with half-hour sessions. Flexibility and experimentation are in order.

The basic principle with respect to duration of counseling is that it continues until either (1) the person being counseled is ready to terminate counseling or (2) the counselor feels nothing is being accomplished or (3) some prearranged date or number of sessions is reached. The latter is known as *time-limited* counseling. There are both practical and theoretical advantages to time-limited counseling. The practical advantage is that it allows the counselor to serve a maximum number of people with his available counseling time. The theoretical advantage is that the knowledge that only a limited number of sessions are available motivates the person to "get down to brass tacks" immediately. Ten to 15 sessions is a common number for time-limited counseling.

Sometimes an open-ended approach is used in which the individual is offered six sessions with an understanding that at the end of that time the counselor and the person will decide together how much longer counseling will continue. Sometimes this turns out to be a time-limited period; sometimes the agreement is to continue until the person is ready to terminate.

Whose Decision?

When counseling is successful, the person comes gradually to a sense of wholeness and personal strength. If it is an unlimited series of sessions, the person eventually begins to talk about the time when it will not be necessary to come for counseling any longer. In time-limited counseling, he usually talks about the fact that the termination date is drawing near and what this means to him. Feelings and thoughts about ending can be as important as any other type of reaction. If the pastor responds to the person's reactions to the termination of counseling, the person is usually able to work through his feelings about ending. It is customary when counseling actually ends for the counselor to "leave a door open." That is, he makes it clear that if the person strongly feels a need to return for additional sessions, he may.

There may be times when the pastor finds it necessary to terminate counseling himself. It may be that he is moving to another congregation. He may feel strongly that counseling is not getting anywhere and that both parties are wasting their time. He may find that the person's problems require referral, or they may repulse him. Under such circumstances the counselor is obligated to give the person a number of sessions to talk through what having counseling terminated means to him. When termination is because the counselor feels the person is too disturbed to go on, specific provision must also be made for referral to another source of aid. It is critical in all these situations that the pastor-counselor be open and honest about his reasons. As difficult as this may seem and as tempting as it may be to invent reasons that will not "hurt" the counselee, he can only harm the person by being less than honest.

Dependency Reactions

Sometimes persons who come for counseling develop a marked dependency on the counselor. The counselor needs to be alert and responsive to cues in the person's manner that would indicate this dependency. The dependency may show up as unwillingness to miss even a single session. It may take the form of asking questions that, if answered, would make the counselor responsible for important decisions. It may appear as a feeling on the counselor's part that counseling is getting nowhere, but the person seems content to keep coming back and talking about the same things again and again. (To specify how to distinguish this from *working through* is not easy, except to say that in working through there is evidence of movement deeper into the problem and increasing self-understanding.) When signs of overdependency occur, they should be dealt with. This can be done by reflecting back to the person those signs that show how dependent he is on counseling—for example, "You find you need these sessions for a sense of well-being," or "I hear you saying you don't see how you could get along without coming here." When the counselor feels inner tension regarding the person's dependency, it may be necessary for him to bring out his own feelings as a means of articulating the relationship.

Some persons, after a termination date has been set, show marked resurgence of symptomatology and problems or an increase in anxiety. This phenomenon can be quite upsetting to the person. It will be for the counselor too if he is not familiar with this possibility and what it means. Last-minute anxiety or return of symptoms appears to be the result of the fact that some dependency is inevitable in counseling. The approaching termination of counseling means that the person will have to go it alone, and this is threatening. The counselor should be prepared to hear the person say, for example, that his old symptoms are back; his problems are worse again; maybe he should keep coming.

Normally, if a closing date for counseling has been set, the pastor should stick with it. This requires, however, a judgment as to whether more counseling sessions really should be arranged or whether this is only a passing phase. A way to handle it is to suggest that counseling be terminated as planned, with the understanding that the person may return if things really become too difficult for him. Another way is to set an additional series of three or four sessions to "taper off" and then terminate. Normally, when counseling has helped the person to greater self-direction, this is all it takes to help him over the hurdle of separation.

After Counseling

The pastor faces a problem that the secular counselor rarely faces. The full-time mental health worker does not ordinarily meet his client or patient in other settings after therapy has ended. The pastor-counselor inevitably meets his counselees in a variety of settings. This raises the question of how the counselor and the person will feel when they meet at the door after church services or at meetings, or when the pastor makes a sick call. As a result of counseling the pastor knows a great deal of very intimate information about the person. The person knows he knows, and as we have seen, what a person thinks other people are thinking can be a prime source of distress.

This is not a new problem for pastors to face. Pastors have always lived with the knowledge of who fights with his wife, who had to get married, who was in trouble with the law, and other privy information. And generally speaking, it is not a serious problem for his parishioners either. People look at the pastor as a professional person and swallow whatever distress this knowledge causes them. The same is true with counseling information except that if the person alludes to any matter that occurred in counseling outside of counseling, the pastor may have to deal with it. The appropriate response is, of course, to reflect the feeling or perception evident in whatever the person says or does—for example, "That problem still bothers you some"; "Sometimes you feel embarrassed in my presence."

Counseling Ethics

One way to talk about counseling ethics is to talk about the *rights of persons counseled*. Most of the rights of persons counseled have been referred to in one way or another in previous pages. It seems worthwhile to summarize them here and then comment on the subjects of confidentiality and supervision.

The Rights of Those Counseled

A person has the right to expect the following from his pastor as a professional counselor:

1. Deep respect for him as a person.
2. The absence of an intimidating or coercive manner in counseling.
3. Sincere efforts to understand and accept him no matter what his problem may be.
4. Willingness to let him explore all his thoughts, feelings, and actions without the counselor showing disapproval or shock.
5. Willingness to let him work out his own solutions in his own way.
6. Concern for his spiritual welfare that transcends any concern the pastor has for the welfare of the church as an institution; that is, willingness to let him make his own decisions even if it means loss to the organized church.
7. Concern for his welfare that transcends any obligations the pastor may feel toward the person's parents, wife, husband, etc.; that is, willingness to let him find his own answers in spite of what other important people may want.
8. Complete confidentiality with respect to information obtained in counseling.
9. Capacity on the part of the counselor to recognize the limits of his own competence.
10. Referral to an appropriate person when the counselor finds it unsuitable to continue counseling.

Confidentiality

Confidentiality is a topic of special concern in counseling. Not only does the welfare of a human being hang on the security of the relationship between the person and the counselor, but a pastor's whole counseling ministry hangs on the question whether he can be trusted not to violate confidential relations. The person has a right to expect complete privacy with respect to the information he divulges during counseling. In fact, no one should ever hear from the pastor who is in counseling. There is reason to believe that some pastors are not always scrupulously discreet about private matters in their congregation. It is quite unthinkable that a pastor would talk about any of the private concerns of his parishioners to his own family or to others, but it is absolutely unthinkable that he would violate counseling confidences. In counseling there is an implicit agreement with respect to confidentiality.

A situation where confidentiality is very likely to become a problem is in counseling with adolescents. Parents feel they have an unlimited right to know what their children are doing and thinking. Some elements within the Christian tradition give support to this idea. One can only point out that if adolescents do not have the right of confidentiality in counseling, they had better be told this at the outset. The chances are that under such circumstances they will not enter counseling, or if they do, only superficial and safe material will be discussed.

There are two instances in which absolute confidentiality may be abrogated. One is when the person is involved in behavior that is obviously so clearly detrimental to his own welfare or society's welfare that he must be protected from himself or society protected from him. Examples include such situations as individuals who are suicidal or homicidal, or where the person is compelling other persons to engage in crime or is setting fires, planning murder, and the like. The other instance is when the person is so clearly mentally disturbed that he must have temporary hospital care.

In both these instances, reporting to the family or to the police should occur only after (1) careful weighing of the question of whether or not action must be taken, (2) confrontation of the individual with the seriousness of the situation and attempts to persuade him to take action *voluntarily,* (3) making it clear to the person that the counselor feels he has no choice but to take appropriate steps, and (4) attempts to make it clear that the counselor still maintains deep regard for the person as a person. Clearly this is a last-resort kind of action and one that will occur extremely rarely.

Supervision

An optimal counseling situation would be one where the pastor receives professional counseling supervision from another professional mental health worker or from a pastor with special professional training.

Supervision in the mental health professions consists of regular meetings with another therapist to talk about the cases the individual is handling. In these meetings a running account of the progress of therapy is given, together with the therapist's evaluations of what is happening. Verbatim conversations from tapes may be examined. The role of the supervisor is to provide a sounding board against which the therapist can project his feelings and ideas about the person. The supervising therapist also helps the therapist discover aspects of the case he is missing and things he may be doing that are hindering the treatment process. Supervision is also, in a sense, therapeutic for the therapist, because it allows him to explore his own feelings about the person and the way treatment is going.

The pastor may be able to strike up a professional relationship with a psychiatrist, clinical psychologist, or social worker for supervision of his counseling. It is not inconceivable that his congregation would pay a professional for such service. In some localities a fully trained psychologist-pastor may be available for supervision. Lacking this opportunity, it may be possible for the pastor to arrange for supervision from a brother pastor, and perhaps he in turn will supervise a third pastor. Such round-robin supervising is common practice in mental health clinics.

Accepting supervision, from whatever source, may be threatening to the pastor-counselor. It is not easy to expose one's "mistakes" and hopes and inner feelings about one's counseling. But it is vital to the welfare of the individuals being counseled and to the pastor's growth as a counselor. If some supervision arrangement is not feasible, the pastor will have to do his counseling without supervision. While this may not preclude counseling, it is not a good situation.

7

Signs of Severe Disorder and Referral

The limits of the pastor's competence for counseling are set (1) by the nature and severity of the person's problem and (2) by the ability and confidence of the pastor himself.

The question of the pastor's ability and confidence is a difficult one to talk about meaningfully. One meets pastors who, from their talk, seem to think they know all there is to know about counseling. Other pastors appear to have so little regard for their abilities as counselors that their first thought is to refer distressed people to another profession or agency. Somewhere between these extremes would seem to lie a more appropriate posture. Most pastors are not well trained for counseling compared to professional mental health workers. There is reason for them to be humble. Yet the demands for counseling are so great that there is a real place for the pastor-counselor who has a sincere desire to help the distressed and an openness to learn. But the point made earlier cannot be repeated too strongly: the pastor has to *work* at developing his own philosophy and method of counseling through reading, through course work, and through practical experience, preferably supervised.

Beyond that the pastor-counselor has another kind of need. He needs to know enough about types and severity of mental disorder to make a judgment as to which persons he can legitimately offer a counseling service and which individuals he should refer elsewhere.

Types of Mental Disorder

Making a judgment about who should be offered counseling requires familiarity with types of mental disorder and a certain minimal ability to judge their severity. Unfortunately we cannot offer here a course in abnormal psychology, but that is the very least that is needed—just to get concepts and terminology clear. To be really skilled at making judgments the counselor would need several years of direct experience with mentally disturbed people in hospitals and clinics to get a "feel" for what the various types of mental disorder are like and the range of their severity. We say *years* advisedly; this is actually what it takes to make a competent diagnostician, and even then diagnosis is difficult business. The difficulty arises from the fact that the recognized mental disorders involve a complex array of symptoms. The symptoms for a given disorder vary from case to case. The symptoms also overlap from one disorder to another.

Nevertheless, for the pastor who has accumulated some knowledge about the various types of mental disorder, it may be helpful to state just where his appropriate sphere of service lies in terms of current categories of disorder. In the table below is a condensed outline showing the main types of mental disorder based on the manual of the American Psychiatric Association.[6] Following it are comments on the pastor's appropriate types of service.

Mental Disorders

Group A

1. *Transient Situational Disorders.* Severe, temporary mental-emotional reactions in otherwise normal individuals due to extreme psychological stress such as is found in war, catastrophes, and other environmental crises. Symptoms usually disappear when stress is removed.

2. *Psychophysiologic Disorders.* Physical illnesses with *actual* tissue changes caused by emotional conflict and psychological

stress. Examples: peptic ulcer, colitis, hypertension, migraine headache. Sometimes called *psychosomatic* disorders. Usually treated as a physical illness rather than as a psychological disorder.

3. *Neuroses.* Severe anxiety from unconscious emotional conflicts experienced either directly as anxiety or in the form of symptoms that symbolize the conflict. Examples: feelings of apprehension or panic for no apparent reason, obsessive thoughts, compulsions, amnesia, phobias, loss of physical functions *without* tissue damage, chronic fatigue, excessive concern about · health, feelings of unreality. Usually do not require hospitalization.

4. *Personality Disorders.* Lifelong patterns of behavior that make the person a moral or social problem. Examples: alcoholism, drug addiction, chronic antisocial behavior, sexual deviations, persistent and extreme expressions of irresponsibility, aggressiveness, immaturity, instability, suspiciousness, or emotional withdrawal. May require hospitalization or may result in incarceration as a legal offender.

5. *Disorders of Childhood and Adolescence.* Reactions in childhood and adolescence involving overactivity, emotional withdrawal, excessive fear or anxiety, excessive aggression, running away, chronic delinquent behavior. Severe "problem" children.

Group B

1. *Psychoses (Functional Psychoses).* Severe emotional and mental disturbance, frequently incapacitating, with marked confusion, withdrawal, or misinterpretation of reality. Not directly caused by any physical condition as far as is known. What most people mean by "mental illness." Require hospitalization during acute phases.

    a. *Schizophrenia.* Marked distortion of thinking, emotions, and actions. Several varieties *(simple, hebephrenic, catatonic, paranoid . . .)* with a broad array of symptoms. Most common of the functional psychoses.

    b. *Affective Disorders.* Disorders of mood. (1) *Involutional Melancholia.* Severe depression, worry, agitation, insomnia occurring for the first time in the involutional period (time of menopause in women, late fifties in men). (2) *Manic-depressive Disorder.* Recurring episodes of mood change involving severe depression or euphoria and overactivity, or both. (3) *Psychotic Reactive Depression.* Severe and incapacitating depression in reaction to an emotional loss, including loss of reality contact.

2. *Organic Brain Disorders (Organic Psychoses).* Mental and emotional disturbance due to changes in brain functioning as a result of disease, injury, deterioration, and other physical causes. Amount of hospital care needed depends on the nature and extent of the disorder.

3. *Mental Retardation.* Inability to adequately care for one's own needs, learn, and exercise judgment due to low intelligence. Caused by inherited or acquired physical factors and by extreme cultural deprivation. Requires custodial care in moderate and severe cases, depending upon degree of impairment.

Psychoses, Brain Disorder, Retardation (Group B)

There is no doubt about the fact that the pastor without highly specialized training has no *counseling* service to offer to individuals with disorders in Group B. The *functional psychoses* (B-1) and the *brain disorders* (B-2) are primarily the province of the psychiatrist and the clinical psychologist. Signs indicative of these kinds of disorders are found in the next section of this chapter. Likewise, the pastor has no "treatment" to offer the person who is *mentally retarded* (B-3), although he may have some help to offer the borderline individual in the way of finding work and learning to get along in society. He may also have some help to offer the family of the retarded in finding special education opportunities or locating custodial care when this is required.

The services of the pastor to individuals in Group B fall under the heading pastoral *care* rather than *counseling.* Nevertheless, this responsibility should not be dismissed lightly. Even though the individual is under the care of a psychiatrist or in a hospital or training school, it does not mean the pastor-counselor has no service to render. He serves the person's spiritual needs through visits, conversation, and witnessing with the Gospel.

Group A Disorders

The pastor's responsibility with respect to disorders in Group A is a different matter. First, it may be noted, the "official" classification system makes no attempt to define normality. This is not mere oversight. The fact is that there is no easy definition of what constitutes "normality." Mental disorder exists on a continuum. At one end are those persons whose problems are so mild that they are accepted by everyone as "normal." Near the same end of the continuum are those whose problems are fairly severe but who function well, sometimes spectacularly, in spite of their conflicts. Often they could profit from help, however. Toward that end of the continuum lies the pastor's primary sphere of legitimate activity. At the other end of the continuum lie the disorders of Group B, discussed above, where the pastor has no counseling responsibility. In between is a borderland made up of the disorders in Group A. Here the pastor's responsibility and his legitimate sphere of activity are not so clear. We will look at these disorders next.

Transient and Psychophysiologic Disorders

The *transient situational disorders* (A-1) and the *psychophysiologic disorders* (A-2) are *primarily* the responsibility of medical people. The transient disorders occur most often as the aftermath of prolonged physical and emotional stress as it is found in war and in catastrophes like earthquakes, conflagrations, and floods. Except for military chaplains, these disorders are unlikely to be seen often by the pastor. While these individuals are temporarily severely incapacitated, they usually respond quickly with minimal care when the pressure is removed. If the pastor has any service to offer them, it is in the form of pastoral care.

However, less severe forms of situational disorder occur. They may follow any emotional crisis, such as a death in the family, serious illness, a divorce, loss of employment, severe failure. The person may be left more impaired in ability to function and for a longer period than people usually take to recover from this kind of experience. The pastor has no doubt seen many instances of this kind of reaction, although he may not have labeled them transient situational reactions. In these cases, if there are no signs of acute mental disorder such as those described in the next part of this chapter, he might offer counseling to help the person work out the meaning of his feelings and reactions. If not counseling, then surely he would provide pastoral care.

Most of the psychophysiologic disorders are handled strictly at a medical level. The ulcer patient lives on a special diet or has surgery; the hypertension (high blood pressure) patient is given drugs; the chronic gastritis (heartburn) patient uses an antacid. Normally the pastor's responsibility to these individuals is that of pastoral care. He visits them when they are in the hospital, and he inquires solicitously about their welfare when they are not, unless they are touchy about the subject.

Occasionally the pastor will encounter individuals with such problems in counseling. Sometimes they seek help with some other, nonmedical problem, and then they reveal that they have a psychophysiologic disorder as well. Sometimes they are advised by their physician to seek help for their emotional conflicts. The physician is not asking the pastor to practice medicine, only to help the individual straighten out his personal problems. In any case, the pastor-counselor should be aware that talking about conflicts can aggravate these physical disorders, in some cases to the point of peril for the person. Normally the pastor should proceed only with the knowledge and advice of the person's physician. He must also be careful not to give the impression he is treating a physical ailment, for that is the practice of medicine. In some cases the pastor may have a responsibility to encourage the person to get medical attention, a legitimate subject either for pastoral care or for confrontation in counseling.

Neurosis and Personality Disorder

It is with the *neuroses* (A-3) and *personality disorders* (A-4) that the issue of what the pastor may legitimately do becomes more complex. Neurotics are individuals whose distortions of reality are not so gross as to make them bizarre or dangerous to themselves or others. Although more severe forms of neurosis may be incapacitating for varying periods of time, the great bulk of neurotic people live with their distress. They are often a burden to those around them because of their chronic complaints, their need for sympathy and support, and their tendency to make others miserable by their emotional distress and their egocentrism. Within this group are those who suffer from anxiety of unknown cause, pseudo physical symptoms, compulsions to go through ritualistic actions, obsessive thoughts they cannot control, phobias of various kinds, preoccupation with their health, and milder forms of depression.

These are the disorders with which the professional mental health workers have had their greatest success using counseling and psychotherapy. In fact, the chief forms of psychotherapy were developed on and for these people. If the pastor attempts counseling with them rather than referral, he may be depriving them of more adequate help. On the other hand, many of these individuals are not inclined to go to a psychiatrist, psychologist, or clinic. With milder problems the pastor may undertake counseling provided he has settled for himself the basic questions concerning his objectives and his competence.

Personality disorders are disorders in which the individual fails to meet society's expectations in the realm of morals and mores. These are people who are chronically irresponsible, unstable, or immoral. Among them are found people who are chronically jobless through their own fault, who fail to pay their debts, who do not provide for their families; people who are actively or passively sadistic toward other people; people who masochistically invite ill treatment from others; people who are addicted to drugs or alcohol; people with a sexual perversion as the dominant feature of their disorder (homosexuals, pederasts, exhibitionists, voyeurists, sexual sadists and masochists).

Is the pastor competent to deal with these kinds of disorders on a counseling basis? The answer may be that it hardly matters whether the pastor is competent or not. These people seldom seek help voluntarily.[7] When they do, or when they are forced to seek help by a court or by pressure from others, treatment is frequently not successful even when it is conducted by the most competent therapists. These are the disorders most resistent to psychotherapy. In the author's opinion, if the pastor can get the individual involved in a counseling relationship, he should do so. He had better be forewarned, however, that he is likely to find himself severely disappointed and frustrated, possibly even exploited.

Disorders of Childhood and Adolescence

Emotional problems of children and adolescents (A-5) come frequently to the pastor's attention. Not many pastors are called upon to do counseling with children, but pastors *are* called upon by parents for advice. If the pastor remembers that *child* psychiatry is a specialty within psychiatry, requiring more training than adult psychiatry, he will perhaps not be tempted to be too free with advice and he will be more inclined to make referrals. Work with adolescents who chronically show excessive anger, uncontrollability, running away, or delinquency is very difficult. They seldom seek help voluntarily. If the pastor can involve the youngster in a relationship, he should try to help him. If that fails, parents should be helped to find other sources of professional help.

These comments about the pastor's appropriate sphere of activity among the recognized types of mental disorder are not meant to be either discouraging or unduly restrictive. They are meant to be realistic and to help the pastor-counselor avoid problems that are outside his professional competence. The primary locus of activity of pastoral counseling (not of pastoral *care,* it should be clear) is with people at the milder end of the distress continuum.

Signs of Severe Disorder

Another way to approach the issue of when to offer counseling is in terms of critical symptoms and severity rather than in terms of conventional categories of disorder. How to judge when the nature or severity of a distressed person's problems lie beyond the competence of the pastor-counselor is not simple to spell out. The following comments are offered as guidelines.

Severe Signs

1. *Physical complaints.* When a distressed person complains of physical symptoms like headaches, body pains, unusual appearance of urine, menstrual flow, bowel movement, mysterious lumps, chronic sore throat, gas pains, or stomach acidity, competent medical examination is necessary. The person should be referred to his own physician with the stipulation that counseling cannot proceed until it is established whether or not an organic disease is involved. The

individual can authorize the physician to tell the pastor whether the problem is largely a medical one or one where counseling is appropriate.

2. *Hallucinations and delusions.* When a person reports experiences that the pastor is reasonably sure have not occurred, the pastor should be very wary and consider immediate referral to a mental health center or to a psychiatrist (or to a physician who can arrange an early appointment with a psychiatrist).

One class of these experiences is *hallucinations.* Hallucinations are sensory experiences for which there is inadequate objective, external stimulus to give rise to the person's experience. Typical hallucinations include hearing voices, hearing strange sounds, seeing persons or things that are not there, seeing "visions," smelling odors (usually foul), experiencing strange tastes or strange skin sensations (for example, that worms are crawling under one's skin). Such experiences are indications of serious mental disorder and possibly of pathological conditions in the brain. One of their characteristic features is that they are so real to the person experiencing them that he cannot believe they do not exist.

Fixed ideas that do not correspond to reality are called *delusions.* They are typically of three broad types. In *delusions of grandeur* the person thinks he is something or someone he is not—for example, Jesus Christ, the President, "All Atomic Power," Satan, Hitler, Stalin, a special government agent. Usually the nature of the delusion is such as to ascribe great power, wisdom, beauty, or evil to the person. Frequently it is a quite transparent attempt on the person's part to compensate for severe inferiority feelings.

In *delusions of persecution* the person feels that things are being done to him by others—people are cheating or stealing from him; they are poisoning his food; his wife is unfaithful; they are plotting against him; they are trying to steal his secrets. Sometimes persons with persecutory delusions become so certain that they are being harmed that they strike out in self-defense. Under these conditions they can become dangerous, even homicidal. Although the number of dangerous cases is really very small, they constitute the kind of risk that cannot be taken lightly.

Delusions of self-derogation are ideas that degrade the person. They may be delusions of great and unforgivable guilt (that one has committed "the sin against the Holy Ghost," for example), delusions of incurable disease, delusions that one's mind or viscera have decayed, delusions that one is absolutely worthless or poverty stricken. Persons with these kinds of delusions sometimes act out their self-directed hostility. They are therefore always potential suicides and must be handled with care.

Very similar to delusional ideas are *ideas of reference*. These are beliefs or suspicions a person has that other people are referring to him in conversation, actions, or gestures when they are not. The person feels he is being laughed at, talked about, pointed to, or watched. In severe form they constitute delusions and are symptomatic of very severe illness. They may be present, however, in mild form in people who are overly concerned about what other people are thinking. How serious such thoughts are depends on how frequently the person has them, how certain he is of their reality, whether his concern about them is great or little, and whether he is inclined to act on the basis of these imagined references.

Sometimes in the course of counseling, a person describes experiences that sound suspiciously delusional or hallucinatory, but one cannot be certain. A person may report sensory experiences or ideas that sound peculiar, but then qualify them by showing that he knows they are only in his mind. When such borderline experiences are reported, the pastor should be cautious. On the one hand, they may be only transitory experiences due to unusual stress of the moment. On the other hand, they may be the precursors of a severe psychotic episode. With respect to referral, the general rule that it is better to be safe than sorry seems to be a wise one.

3. *Disorientation for time, place, person, circumstance.* People who are disoriented for time, place, person, and circumstance are clearly beyond the pastor's counseling competence. That is, the person who is confused about the month or year or who thinks he is living in a different time, the person who doesn't know where he is or thinks he is some place where he is not, the person who thinks he is someone else or who is confused about who he is, and the person who is mute and will not respond to questions are in need of immediate psychiatric care.

4. *Mental confusion.* Thought processes can be disturbed and confused in many ways. When the pastor encounters a person who seems to be dazed, disorganized, delirious, stuporous, or excessively sleepy or who seems to slip in and out of consciousness, immediate medical evaluation is needed. When a person seems to move from one train of thought to another without any indication that a transition is being made, a warning signal ought to flash in the pastor's mind. This sort of "looseness" in thought progression can often be detected, because the counselor has a distinct feeling of bewilderment as to how they suddenly got to a different topic. He may even wonder whether it was his own mind that slipped a cog.

Almost the opposite can also be a significant sign. If the person repeats the same idea over and over and never progresses in his train of thought, that is, if he *perseverates*, he is in serious difficulty. If a person talks in disconnected and meaningless phrases, "word salad" it has been called, or if he seems incoherent or jumps rapidly from idea to idea and can't slow down when asked, he is showing severe pathology.

Gross disturbances in memory, especially those where

the individual tries to cover up his memory loss with a fabrication, are symptoms of brain damage or severe mental disorder. (These lapses should not be confused with minor instances of forgetting, which almost everyone experiences and which often frighten the anxious person into thinking there is something wrong with his mind.)

5. *Inappropriate affect.* When a person's mood does not fit the objective circumstances, it is at least a sign of emotional stress. When the inappropriateness of affect becomes severe or persistent—for example, if a person continues to laugh when he should be sad or weep when he should be happy—there is an indication that something is seriously wrong. This, of course, does not refer to people who become a little weepy at a wedding, or give a little laugh of anxiety in a moment of tension or sadness. It refers to people who appear happy or unconcerned in a circumstance where others would be sad or worried. It refers to people who are chronically sad or abjectly depressed when there is no objective reason to feel that way.

Very severe *depression,* in which a person will not talk, does not eat, seems to be in another world, bemoans his fate, talks of suicide, or describes morbid thoughts, is very serious. So also is *agitation,* in which a person constantly wrings his hands, paces the floor, complains of inner turmoil, appears anguished, or acts irrational.

Two signs of severe depression that are not always recognized are weight loss due to lack of interest in food and waking up in the early hours of the morning and being unable to go back to sleep. (Inability to go to sleep when one goes to bed is usually a neurotic sign and is less serious.) Equally serious is false euphoria, or *mania,* in which the person appears to be in a fiesta mood or wildly elated for no appropriate reason.

An *absence of appropriate feeling* can be equally significant.

In this case the person appears "flat," or empty of feeling. Often it is accompanied by withdrawal from social relationships as an added sign.

6. *Bizarre behavior.* When individuals exhibit peculiar or outlandish behavior it *may* be a sign of severe disorder. For example, individuals who appear to talk to imaginary persons, go out or threaten to go out unclothed, act silly in inappropriate situations, dress in bizarre ways, use strange gestures as if to ward off unwanted voices or visions, or act as if they are badly frightened when there is no objective cause should be carefully evaluated.

7. *Destructive acts and threats.* Persons who threaten to harm others or themselves must be treated very seriously no matter how much they may later protest that they were only kidding or that they no longer have such ideas. If they have actually acted out any suicidal or assaultive threats, it is doubly serious. Thus people who brandish guns or knives, pretend they are going to strangle or bludgeon someone else, go into violent states of rage, talk about doing destructive things, or are preoccupied with morbid, destructive ideas constitute a serious problem.

If the hostility is turned upon self in the form of making suicide attempts (like swallowing pills, cutting the wrists, or threatening to jump off a high place or hang themselves), this should not be taken lightly. A proportion of these persons will eventually take their own life.

Adults who physically abuse small children, resulting in what has been called the "battered child syndrome," must be reported to the authorities, preferably by a relative. The child is in mortal danger.

8. *Counselor discomfort.* Another type of sign should also be heeded. A counselor's *level of uneasiness* can be a good barometer of the seriousness of a person's condition. A good rule of thumb is that when the counselor feels uncomfortable

about a person's mental condition, it's time for referral or to get an independent professional opinion. The pastor should trust his own feelings of discomfort.

Less severe signs

There are a number of signs of mental disorder that generally connote a less critical situation than those above. They usually fall in the area of neurotic symptomatology. Consequently, the considerations noted above about counseling with neurotics apply to persons showing these characteristics.

1. *Anxiety and fear.* The person may be showing signs of diffuse, "free floating," anxiety. This may range from mild general apprehensiveness to acute panic. These feelings appear for no apparent reason, and the person may fear he is "losing his mind." If the person appears to be in good contact with reality, is logical, and otherwise shows no suspicious signs of severe disorder, it is probably neurotic anxiety.

When the person's anxiety is centered on some particular object or circumstance, he is said to be *phobic*. The fear may be of small, enclosed places like elevators or corridors (claustrophobia). It may be of high places (acrophobia) or unfamiliar places where people congregate (agoraphobia). The fear may be of objects like snakes, knives, rats. Some individuals experience phobic reactions in church or in connection with Holy Communion. These phobias are usually neurotic manifestations unless more severe signs accompany them.

2. *Obsessions and compulsions.* Obsessions are ideas that come to a person unbidden and can't be eliminated from the mind at will. They are disturbing to the individual because they are usually of a useless, vulgar, or profane sort. Thus the person has thoughts with sexual, hostile, or senseless content. They come into the mind like a flash, and they are quite upsetting. For example, a student wondered every time he looked at a crucifix whether Christ had an erection. Again, assuming

the absence of other signs of severe disorder, this is likely to be neurotic. Fleeting thoughts of suicide (as opposed to preoccupation, actual planning, and suicide attempts) fall in the same category.

In other instances the person may feel a *compulsion* to carry out various acts like touching or counting certain things or people, always doing things in a precise, ritualistic order, doing things a specific number of times (like locking and unlocking the door three times). Compulsions to keep everything neat, orderly, and immaculate followed by emotional upset when they are not are fairly common. Often obsessions and compulsions go together.

3. *Hypochondriacal concerns.* Some individuals are preoccupied with their health. They examine their tongues every morning, observe their urine and stools for unusual color, keep a record of their bowel movements, or listen to their heartbeat constantly. They worry about their health excessively, and often they run to their physician until they drive the poor man to distraction. They have medicine closets full of pills and potions. Usually these are signs of neurotic anxiety, but if there are specific physical complaints, they should be checked by a physician.

4. *Reactive depression.* When a person is excessively depressed, or depressed *and* agitated, it is a serious matter. But some individuals become depressed to a more moderate degree. In these instances the depression does not interfere with their usual pursuits to the point of incapacitation, although it may reduce their effectiveness somewhat. Usually the depression can be traced to an actual loss in the person's life. Because it is a reaction to a specific occurrence like a death in the family, loss of job, or failure, it is said to be a *reactive* depression. While the counselor should proceed with caution, such depressions are not necessarily beyond his competence if there are no other signs of severe disorder.

Referral Resources

The pastor-counselor must make judgments about which distressed people are beyond his competence. His next need is to know to whom he can refer individuals who require help from another profession.

Private practitioners

Many members of the full-time mental health professions are in private practice. Psychiatrists can be found in the yellow pages of the telephone book under *Physicians* or through the physicians' telephone exchange, but probably the best source of names is through one's own physician. Clinical psychologists will be listed in the yellow pages under *Psychologists,* if there are any in private practice. For persons with a serious mental disorder, a *clinical* rather than a *counseling* psychologist is needed. Those psychologists with the notation *ABPP Diplomate* after their names have the highest certification of competence their profession gives. There are relatively few psychiatric social workers in private practice, but a trend toward private practice appears to be developing.

In some localities several psychiatrists or several psychologists practice as a group, and sometimes psychiatrists, psychologists, and social workers combine skills as a group. The fees of private practitioners are, of course, generally substantially higher than those of public agencies.

Agencies

It is impossible to list all the different kinds of agencies that offer help to the distressed. They are many and varied, and they carry a bewildering array of names. We will look briefly at (1) agencies that deal primarily with mental disorder and (2) agencies that help people with problems that do not involve mental disorder.

1. *Mental health facilities.* Agencies specifically designed to aid in mental health problems include the following:

The *child guidance clinic* has become a national institution in America. Child guidance clinics first began to make their appearance after the turn of the century as a part of the mental hygiene movement, a movement to promote a better understanding of the mentally ill, better treatment, and preventive mental health care. The staffs of these agencies ordinarily consist of a psychiatrist-director, clinical psychologists, and social workers. They are usually supported by public contributions, fees, and subsidy from local government. Such agencies work in cooperation with welfare boards, courts, schools, and other social agencies. They offer outpatient psychotherapy and counseling to parents and children. Sometimes they recommend environmental manipulation like foster home placement or change of school. Work with the parents of a disturbed child is considered essential, and most clinics will not attempt to treat a child unless at least one of the parents can be treated also.

Adult psychiatric clinics are also becoming common. Most of them are modeled after child guidance clinics (psychiatrist-director, clinical psychologists, social workers, community financial support, and a team approach). Their services are usually offered only on an outpatient basis. Fees are geared to the person's ability to pay.

Mental hospitals assist primarily those persons whose mental disorder requires custodial care in a hospital setting. About half of the approximately 500 mental hospitals in the United States are state and county hospitals. The other half are small private "sanitoriums" (about 200) and federal government hospitals (less than 50). Admission to private hospitals is voluntary and is arranged through a physician. Admission to federal hospitals, like the VA hospitals, is also voluntary, but the individual must qualify for admission.

Admission to a state or county mental hospital may be requested by the person himself. More frequently it is voluntary admission following persuasion by physician or family. Legal commitment by court order on the recommendation of physicians is becoming less frequent.

Many general medical hospitals now have *psychiatric wards*. These offer specialized services for relatively short-term treatment of acute mental disorder. They have the distinct advantage of not requiring removal of the individual from his community and not putting him into the frightening confines of a mental hospital. However, if the person does not respond to treatment within several weeks, he will usually be removed to a mental hospital.

The latest development in resources for the treatment of mental disorder, and undoubtedly *the* facility of the future, is the broad-range *community mental health center*. These centers, which are developing across the country, are being given initial financial support by the federal government on a matching-funds basis. They provide child and adult service, inpatient and outpatient service, and special services like vocational guidance and vocational rehabilitation. Some offer such novel arrangements as day care for people who need help in the daytime but can spend their nights at home and night care for people who can go to work or take care of themselves during the day but not at night.

2. *Other sources of help.* There are a variety of agencies that help people who have a problem but who do not have significant mental disorder. We will describe briefly a few key types.

Vocational guidance for those who need help in selecting a vocation and finding appropriate educational experiences is provided by a number of different agencies. Guidance officers in schools give aptitude and interest tests and assist students to choose an occupation and school program to suit their interests and abilities. They also assist in the selection of trade schools and colleges and help the student apply.

Almost every college and university provides a guidance service for its students. They help the student select courses, resolve questions about vocational choice, acquire better study and reading habits, and find financial help. Often these services are available to nonstudents as well.

The Veterans Administration offers guidance service to veterans. The United States Employment Service offers limited service to people seeking employment. Special agencies work with the physically disabled, the deaf, the blind, and other handicapped persons.

Marriage counseling centers are becoming common in larger communities. They employ psychologists and social workers and may retain a psychiatrist's services on a consulting basis. Many social service agencies (see below) include marital counseling in their activities. There are many private marriage counselors, but in some places the field is rife with incompetents and charlatans, so referral must be made with great caution.

Welfare agencies exist to help persons with financial needs. There is some kind of department of public welfare in every state, in almost every city, and in most counties. Welfare agencies provide temporary aid in emergencies and longer-term financial assistance in cases where the wage earner of a family is missing or incapacitated. They may help the family obtain aid from social security, unemployment insurance, or disability funds, and they disburse funds from their own accounts.

Public and private children's institutions exist in most communities to care for neglected, orphaned, emotionally disturbed, mentally retarded, and delinquent children. Each institution has its own characteristics. Most have a clearly defined policy as to what kinds of problems they will handle, in what age range, and for how long. In most communities such institutions must be licensed to operate and inspected periodically.

Legal aid societies exist in many communities to assist persons with legal problems. If the individual can't afford to pay, free or inexpensive legal aid is supplied by members of the local bar association. These societies try particularly to protect the legal rights of children and persons who are exploited or abused. Providing legal counsel in criminal proceedings is, however, usually the responsibility of the court that is hearing the case.

The term *social service agency* covers a wide variety of organizations with an extensive array of purposes. Many of the above are social service agencies. There are agencies to deal with child and family welfare problems, including neglect and cruelty. Some provide service to unmarried mothers, adoption service, and foster home placement. They may supply homemaker service to families where the mother is absent or incapacitated. Some provide marriage counseling and personal counseling. They are staffed primarily by social workers.

The work of some agencies is supported by religious groups. Very often they bear a name that clearly indicates their denominational affiliation – Lutheran Social Service, Catholic Charities and Social Service, United Jewish Services. If there is a local social service agency of his denomination, the pastor will undoubtedly want to become acquainted with its services and its personnel, because he will have frequent occasion to make referrals and ask for consultation.

Making Referrals

Knowing the Resources

One of the marks of a competent professional person is that he knows where to send people he himself cannot help.

Every family doctor has a list of surgeons, internists, ophthalmologists, and other specialists to whom he refers individuals. The lawyer knows who the technical legal specialists are in his community. The same knowledge of where to refer people should characterize the pastor.

The pastor needs to know who does what in his community. How can he find out? The answer seems too simple to put on paper. The way to find out is to *ask*. He can ask other local pastors to whom they refer parishioners. He can ask his physician or call a social agency he does know. He will soon learn which agencies help the unwed mother, care for the mentally retarded, give vocational guidance tests, provide economic assistance to the destitute, and offer psychological help.

Many communities publish a booklet showing all the services offered by local social service agencies, schools, courts, community centers, and the like. The place to ask whether such a directory exists is at a social work agency, at the city or county welfare office, or at the local chamber of commerce. Such a directory covers everything from adoption service to X ray.

Not only does the pastor need to know who does what, he needs to know how well and with what basic attitudes. Blind referral is not advocated. Simple competence is an issue. Not every psychiatrist, psychologist, or agency can be assumed to be as good as every other. Sometimes it is necessary to learn from hard experience, but usually word gets around as to which professional men and agencies are topflight and which are not. If the pastor is a circumspect man and becomes acquainted with physicians, psychologists, and social workers, he can usually get a pretty direct answer as to whom these people think are the best in the community. They may be reluctant to say anything critical about members of their own group, professional ethics being what they are, but they will readily point to the better people.

The other basic consideration in making referrals is the attitudes held by the person or agency to whom referral may be made. Of particular importance are attitudes about Christianity and religious belief. This is especially critical when a person is being referred for some type of psychotherapy or counseling. A pastor can't, in good conscience, refer a parishioner to a psychiatrist or psychologist who takes an actively negative attitude toward religious commitment. Such persons are the exception rather than the rule, but they do exist. Openly confessing Christian practitioners are equally rare.

Most often the pastor will have to settle for a professional person who takes a nonjudgmental, permissive attitude toward religious questions. Fortunately, this is the prevailing attitude in the mental health professions today. That is, the person's right to his own beliefs is respected regardless of what the therapist believes or thinks personally. The role of the therapist is to help the person determine his own beliefs and philosophy, not to impose a belief system on him.

Nevertheless, the pastor still has an obligation to know something about the people to whom he makes referrals. It is not farfetched to think that the pastor will go out of his way to meet the professional people to whom he expects to refer parishioners. He can arrange to have lunch with a psychiatrist or visit the director of a social agency staff. A professional person will usually resent direct questioning about his attitudes, as if he were somehow on public trial, but if the pastor is open about his concerns, a two-way exchange will usually follow in which both parties form impressions of the other. If such an exchange is resented or refused, the pastor has probably learned what he needs to know and he had better look further. If the exchange is fruitful, both parties may have gained an ally and a resource for their professional work.

Making a Referral

Making a referral is fairly simple. The pastor tells the distressed person that he does not believe he is in a position to help him directly but thinks help from someone else is needed. He then gives the person the name of the person or agency he believes could help. He suggests that the person call for an appointment. Since this is a part of pastoral care, he can be fairly direct about it, but he may find it important to explore with the person how he feels about getting help. If the person indicates unwillingness, the pastor may very well reflect this fear or hesitancy. When the situation is not critical, it is the person's right to decide not to seek further help. If the situation is critical, persuasion may be needed.

Normally the pastor does not pick up the phone and make an appointment for the person. If an appointment is to be made, it should be done by the person or by a member of the family. In some instances the pastor may wish to call the professional person or agency, however, and let it be known that he is referring such and such a person.

The question of how much feedback the pastor can expect from the referral source is hard to answer. Psychiatrists, psychologists, and social agencies have the same strict attitudes about divulging information about their clients that one assumes the pastor has. Usually, sharing of information does not extend beyond their own profession or agency. Yet the pastor has an understandable desire to know how a person is doing and what, if any, special considerations the professional person thinks should govern his relation with the person.

The first concern, the pastor's desire to know how the person is doing, may go unrewarded, since not many professional people will be inclined to give a progress report. The second concern, what the pastor needs to keep in mind in dealing with the person, may be more readily forthcoming.

Nevertheless, the pastor can expect to meet with everything from blunt refusal to say a word to mutual cooperation from his referral resources. Much will depend on how they size him up, whether or not they see him as nosy, judgmental, trustworthy, professionally capable, and the like. Nothing can substitute for the pastor making deliberate efforts to get to know the people to whom he makes referrals and building up a relationship of mutual respect.

Emergency Situations

Sometimes it happens that the pastor finds himself in a real emergency with a mentally disturbed person. The person's family or direct observation makes it clear that immediate help is needed. For example, the person is clearly psychotic. If the emergency is extreme, that is, if the person appears dangerous to himself or to others, it may be necessary to call the police or the fire department. This is true, for example, in instances where a person is assaultive, is threatening with a knife or gun, or is about to attempt suicide. In less extreme situations it is better to call a physician, who can make arrangements for local hospitalization, call in a psychiatrist, or arrange for commitment to a mental hospital.

But, and this is a significant point, the calling of the police, fire department, or physician should be done by someone who has legal responsibility for the person, not by the pastor. Normally this is a parent, guardian, husband, wife, brother, or sister. Only in the rarest cases will the pastor wish to assume this responsibility. Whenever possible, of course, it is best to have the person refer himself to an appropriate agency.

8

The Pastor as a Person

The way people perceive the pastor is significant for whether or not they will ever come for counseling and how safe they will feel about counseling. Therefore the pastor's whole professional life, and at times even his private life, are related to his counseling.

The pastor is in a position different from the typical professional mental health worker. The pastor sees people in a variety of contexts – at meetings, at church services, even socially. The psychiatrist, psychologist, and social worker see the people with whom they do therapy only for that purpose and during scheduled hours. What kinds of persons they are outside of the therapeutic hour has little effect on the client or patient. But every move the pastor makes, from the way he preaches to the way he treats his children, can have an effect on whether or not people will come to him for help. It isn't, however, only what he says and does but what he *is* that is important. What he says and does is a reflection of what *he is as a person.* Consequently, we focus in our last chapter on the pastor as a person.

At this point we also recombine the issues of pastoral care and pastoral counseling. For what we have to say about the pastor as a person applies to the pastor in his everyday professional relationships and to pastoral care as well as to the special relationship that is counseling. Indeed, it is even pertinent to his personal life with his family and friends, although we will not go into that area.

Our concern here is with (1) further amplification of the idea of the pastor as a perceptive, empathizing human being, (2) an examination of the pastor as a person who plays various *roles,* and (3) the pastor's own faith and his use of the Word. There are, of course, many other necessary and desirable characteristics of the pastor listed in Scripture and discussed in the literature of pastoral theology, but these we will not consider for lack of space.

The Empathic Pastor

The pastor at his best ought to be a perceptive, *empathizing* human being as he meets distressed people—whether in counseling or in pastoral-care situations. That is to say, he ought to be a person who responds in depth to the experiences of others.

This responding is not mere intellectual recognition of the experiences of the other person. It is not enough merely to be able to say, "He is happy," or "She is worried," as if one were making only a statement of fact. Needed is an understanding of the other person in which the pastor himself *feels* some of what the other person is experiencing. The technical word for it in psychology is *empathy (Einfühlung).* It is a "feeling into" the experiences of the other person. It is a response with the whole self that has physical as well as mental qualities. Empathic responding involves subtle changes in blood pressure, muscle tension, and emotions as the pastor struggles to understand the other person's experience. It can be likened to "crawling into the other person's world" for a brief moment.

It can be asked: Is that really possible? Can one person really experience, even for a moment, what another person is going through? The answer is, Only to a degree. A wise observer put it this way: "No man can ever know what it is like to have a baby." It is impossible for a male to experience with any completeness the fear, pain, relief, and, for many women, the joy and fulfillment of giving birth. It is not possible to get fully into that world. Yet it is possible for a sensitive husband who is allowed into the labor room to know and feel something of his wife's experience as she groans and grunts and digs her nails into his hand when the pains come. And after she returns from the delivery room, it is possible to catch some of her exhaustion, relief, and happiness. In the same way it is possible to experience to a degree the grief, pain, loneliness, relief, or happiness of another human being in counseling or pastoral care.

The first requirement is that two people be in actual contact with each other. Little in the way of empathic understanding can go on through letters or through reports from other people. That is one reason why it is fruitless to try to do counseling by letter or through a third party. The real flavor of what is happening inside a person is lost when people are that remote. A telephone conversation is only little better. Too many of the nuances of behavior are absent in a telephone conversation—facial expression, body position, muscle tension. Empathic understanding requires face-to-face contact.

A second necessary ingredient is an *intended* sensitivity to what the other person is communicating. Such sensitivity amounts to a conscious and deliberate attempt to find out what the other person is experiencing. It calls for a stance in which the listener is in effect asking: "What is he really feeling? What is he really saying? What is the emotional experience behind the words, the gestures, the posture, the facial expression?"

The latter suggests that what a person is saying in words is not necessarily what he is feeling. That can be all too true. A little observation will reveal that it is not uncommon to find a person telling how he enjoyed something, while his face registers displeasure. Sometimes a person will talk about misfortune or loss with a smile on his face. It is very common to find a person saying he is interested when his manner suggests boredom, or that he is happy when his expression suggests distress. The pastor needs to be open to all the cues coming in from other people.

A Phenomenological Approach

Vital to an empathic understanding of people in distress is an approach that may be called *phenomenological*. In this approach the goal of the perceiver is not to understand the other person from the perceiver's point of view or from some presumed objective viewpoint, but to understand the other person from that person's own point of view. The idea is that how a person experiences the phenomena of his own life, that is, how he sees himself and his world, *is* his reality. It is the only reality he knows or can know at any given moment.

This is not the place to enter into a discussion of the nature of objective reality. The important point is that how one person sees things may not be the same as the way another person sees them. In some cases this difference may be evidence of severe mental disorder, but the bulk of such discrepancies are not grossly pathologic. For example, a man sees his son as a better ballplayer than the coach sees him. A small child thinks a penny is better than a dime because it is bigger. A woman depreciates her cooking more than is warranted. A man worries about whether he has cancer when he does not. This is the phenomenal world of others that the pastor needs to understand. He even has to feel the way the other person feels to a degree — sad, happy, anxious, fearful.

Adopting a phenomenological perspective does not require the pastor to abdicate reason. He does not have to believe in the reality of others with the same sureness that the other person does. There are situations in which the perceived world of another person is completely out of accord with reality as the pastor sees it. No one else would agree with the person's version of reality either. The hallucinations or delusions of a severely disturbed person are examples. The pastor is not expected to hear voices or believe there is a plot against the person. He can be expected, however, to believe that the other person has such experiences and that they are very real and disturbing to him. He can even be expected to catch brief glimpses of how things must seem to this disturbed person. In a sense, the pastor has to stand with one foot in his own reality and one foot in the other person's reality.

This capacity to enter partially into the experience of another person is vital for *all* a pastor's professional activities. He needs, for example, to sense momentarily the anxiety of a person facing surgery, the helplessness of a man who has just lost his wife, the mixed emotions of an adolescent who is revolting against family controls. The pastor needs to be able to put himself briefly into the pews on Sunday morning and sense what the worshipers may be experiencing – the quiet desperation of a person who has come to church for the first time in years, the utter boredom of the person for whom church is just a ritual, the impatience of the youngsters who wiggle and squirm, the pleasant calm of those who are in no hurry at all to leave the house of the Lord.

He needs to be just as empathic about the manner in which people react in public situations – to sense the honest concern of the man who disagrees with the way things are being done in the church; to feel some of the healthy outburst of energy of the youngsters as they literally explode out of school; to sense the annoyance and disdain of his critics in the congregation. In short, he has to be perceptive of what's really going on in other people.

Responding to Experience Outside of Counseling

How the pastor should respond when he senses what other people are experiencing, especially when it is negative, is another question. One of the things he can do is to *reflect* the experience the person is expressing. In other words, reflection is not a response that must be restricted only to counseling. It will be used less frequently outside of counseling, but there are many appropriate places for the pastor to deliberately reflect what another person is expressing about his thoughts, feelings, and actions.

One place is at the sickbed. Too much of what people do in the face of sickness and death is devoted to trying to suppress the feelings a seriously sick person has. The family and medical personnel, because it makes them anxious, try to talk the sick person out of his fears and concerns rather than deal with them openly. But the pastor in his visits may very well want to reflect—"You're worried about how the children are getting along without you," or "You're afraid you're not going to get well." He should, of course, be prepared to follow this up with further reflections and with *gentle confrontation* with the Word of God.[8]

Another place to use reflection is in dealing with adolescents. If the cues warrant, he may reflect: "You're pretty dissatisfied with our youth program," or "Sometimes you do what the others are doing even though you don't really want to." Nor need all the pastor's out-of-counseling reflections be concerned with unpleasant experiences. He may want to reflect to the parent whose son has just graduated from college, "This is a happy day for you." Or he may reflect to the man who has just had a promotion, "You're really on top of the world right now." He may reflect ambivalences—"There are things you like about me as your pastor and things you don't like."

One word of caution should be added, however. Reflection of a person's reactions in the presence of other people can be acutely embarrassing. The fact is that much of the time people in our society don't face their true feelings. Their experiences are expressed in what they say and do, but they don't recognize the feeling behind those words and actions. Thus for the pastor to say, "You're bored with all this," can bring anything from nervous laughter to vigorous denial, especially if there are other people present. The reflection then acts as an accusation and is threatening.

We are not saying the pastor should never use reflection when other people are around, but he must be sensitive to its possible effects. He should also be prepared to reflect further any reactions he gets — for example, "I made you uncomfortable by calling attention to the fact you're bored," "It's difficult to acknowledge that you're annoyed with me." Clearly, judicious use of reflection is called for outside of counseling. Nevertheless, the use of reflection in out-of-counseling situations is one of the ways the pastor can show his capacity for empathic understanding and his concern for people and their problems. If he does and if he is truly an understanding and accepting person, it will increase the likelihood that people will come to him for help when they are in distress.

Permissiveness and Directiveness in Pastoral Care

The question of permissiveness versus directiveness in pastoral care must be reopened briefly. As the pastor deals with people who are *not* offered counseling — and they form the bulk of his work with distressed people — how directive can or should he be?

In everyday contacts with distressed people the pastor can afford to be more directive, in the sense of offering suggestions, persuading, comforting, and consoling, than he is in counseling. The pastor has to judge on the basis of the individual and the circumstances whether he will take a more directive or a relatively nondirective approach. He judges on the basis of (1) his estimate of the person's ability to handle his problem by himself, (2) the person's past successes and failures in coping with his problems, and (3) the nature of the problem.

People should be allowed to work out their own solutions to problems as much as possible. But situations may arise in which the pastor believes it is both legitimate and desirable to intervene. He may tell the overly dependent wife to stop running to Mama for sympathy every time she and her husband have a spat, and he may warn Mama that she is a menace to her daughter's marriage. He may guide a person toward problem solution or call attention to an aspect of God's Word of which the person is unaware. When a person has a question, he may tell him the answer or direct him to where the answer may be found. In short, in pastoral care the pastor is a *pastor*—that is, a shepherd, a leader, who immediately and directly brings God's Word into action to alleviate human distress and who uses whatever other methods seem appropriate in a particular situation. This, it is assumed, is what pastors have always done.

Two warnings are in order. First, the pastor ought never to put himself in the position of siding with vested interests. For example, if he wishes to maintain the respect and confidence of young people, the pastor had better not be found constantly aligning himself with parents and with authority. In marriage problems he'd better not side with either party. In congregation disagreements he had better not always be a defender of the status quo.

The second warning is that the pastor had better not let concern for the church as an institution come before his concern for people. Too often pastors worry more about attendance figures, contributions, and public relations than they worry about the human beings involved. Suggesting that blacks should attend a "colored church," catering to Mr. and

Mrs. Uppity while neglecting the Gotnot family, and shaming people into church attendance are examples of situations where the pastor is tempted to sell his spiritual responsibility for the pottage of institutional preservation. People do not feel safe with a pastor of this sort. Without a feeling of safety, there can be no counseling *or* effective pastoral care.

The Pastor's Roles

The pastor needs to be not only empathic in his understanding of people, he must also be a human being of *integrity.* By this is meant that, insofar as he can, the pastor has to be completely honest about himself and his own inner experiences. It may seem strange to suggest that pastors, who are supposed to be society's exemplars of virtue, need to be cautioned to be honest. Nevertheless, it is true. The kind of dishonesty referred to here is not that of deliberate lying or deceiving. Although clergy are not immune to such deceit, that is not where the problem lies. The problem lies in the *roles* the pastor is tempted to play. These are roles that are socially acceptable, that seem to be demanded of him, but that are contrary to his true inner experience. Playing such roles can be dishonest.

An elaboration of what *role-playing* means is required. Every human being plays several roles in life. The first thing to get clear is that role-playing, in the psychological sense of the word, does not necessarily imply hypocrisy or deception. It refers to the fact that every person acts in accord with the way he thinks he ought to act in each new situation. The salesman is a somewhat different person with a customer than he is with the boss, and still a different person when he is bowling with his team. The housewife is a different person when she is talking with the school principal than when she talks to her 3d-grader or to her husband. These are not deliberate falsifications. They are appropriate behavior patterns suited to the circumstance. In fact, people who cannot shift roles appropriately may be mentally disturbed.

Role Sources

The pastor plays, or is expected to play, several roles. These roles derive from numerous sources. Some aspects of the pastor's roles derive from his self-concept. For example, he believes he is sympathetic, warm, understanding, so he acts the way he thinks a sympathetic, warm, understanding person would act. He tries to show interest and concern, or he expresses sympathy, as the situation warrants. Some aspects of the roles the pastor plays derive from his life situation. He is a father and husband, so he acts the way he thinks a father and husband should or would act; he is firm with his children, loving to his wife, ready to give advice to younger men.

Some aspects of the roles he plays derive from his concept of a minister. He thinks ministers are dealing with holy matters so he acts holy and pious, sometimes to the point of overacting. For example, he believes ministers should be against sin, so he frowns appropriately whenever he hears a vulgar or profane word. Some aspects of the roles he plays derive from what he thinks others are thinking and expect. He believes the parishioners expect him to attend all the softball games of the church league, so he does. He believes they expect him to be cheerful and smiling, so he is, regardless of how he feels. Some aspects of the roles he plays may even derive from the behavior of his predecessor. When he first came to St. Swithin's, they told him that the former pastor never said a word about salary raises, so he is reluctant to broach the matter with his church council.

The Hazards of Roles

Now the question is, What is wrong with role-playing for the pastor? How does it become a hazard in his relationships with people? The answer is that role-playing tends to interfere with empathic understanding when it requires the pastor to be something he is not. If a person is busy being something he is not, this interferes with sensitive listening and willingness to see things from another person's perspective. In addition, if role-playing gets very far from the person's real feelings and attitudes, this is soon sensed by others. He is judged by them to be "putting on a front" or "just going through the motions" or even "phony."

Some ministers seriously decrease their effectiveness with people this way. They exude Christian piety with such intensity that they are immediately written off as too pious, too holy to understand how normal people feel. Or they appear so full of concern for others that the person is afraid of being overwhelmed with goodness and concern. In nonprofessional relationships some of this can be tolerated by people, or it can be escaped. In professional relationships it is a detriment to good pastoral care, and in counseling it is absolutely deadly.

There is a genuine paradox here. On the one hand, role-playing is a natural and necessary type of behavior. On the other hand, whenever the pastor plays a role that is contrary to his true feelings and wishes, this will tend to spoil the quality of his relationships with people and decrease his effectiveness.

But that is only the beginning of the problem. The problem is even more complex for the pastor, more so than for the psychologist or psychiatrist, because as a Christian the pastor *is* committed to filling a role that is contrary to his nature. He is committed to living the Good Life, the moral life, when by nature he is, like all other men, self-centered and sinful. Most mental health professionals are only committed to living like decent human beings. And technically they are only committed to being decent human beings during office hours. In contrast the pastor has taken on, and he has had ascribed to him by others, the role of an exemplar of the faith.

Two aspects of the problem can be isolated. One is the temptation to play roles that are alien to the pastor's real feelings and are thus fraudulent. The other is that, as a Christian, the pastor is committed to filling a role that is not entirely natural for him. We will look at each in turn.

Openness to Self

The first part of the problem, the temptation to fill alien roles, can be viewed this way. To begin, the pastor need not feel too distressed when he recognizes that he is tempted to play roles that do not fit him. This is true for everyone, and in this sense he is certainly not peculiar, different, or bad.

Second, it is a matter of recognizing the temptation to be something he is not. This is an area where, to a large extent, knowledge can be power. If the pastor is open to his own inner experiences, if he can recognize the temptation to pretend to be holier than he is, to rule his congregation like a despot, or to hide the fact that as an adolescent he wasn't much different than his own teen-agers, then the battle is half won. If he can acknowledge to himself that he fights with his wife, that he gives attractive women the once-over, that he sometimes uses vulgar or profane language under his breath, that some Sunday mornings he would just as soon not go to church, that sick calls are hard for him, or that he plays up to the automobile dealer in his congregation, this acknowledgment alone will reduce the likelihood of his playing a fraudulent role. The reason for this is that most people can't tolerate incongruity within themselves. They can't put on a front of piety and perfection when inside they know what they are really like.

The temptation to hide one's true nature is not limited to morally or socially disapproved behavior. It can happen with socially approved behavior as well. The pastor can feel that he is too generous and, in bending over backward to avoid cloying generosity, act uncharitable. Or he can be afraid of being overemotional and be artificially restrained, or of being too sympathetic and put on a cloak of professional aloofness. He may even act less pious than he is to make people think he's human. It all depends on how he perceives himself in relation to others.

The pastor needs self-knowledge, and getting this kind of self-knowledge takes effort. It requires adopting an attitude of ruthless honesty in which no aspect of self is hidden or denied. Such a level of inner knowledge can't really be attained completely, of course. Everyone is deceived about himself to some extent because of motivational factors that are out of awareness (unconscious). By their very nature they cannot be made known by a simple act of will. Yet the man who offers himself to the public as a professional helper of the distressed can be expected to work at being better acquainted with himself than average, and a player of alien roles to a degree less than average. This is part of what it means to lay claim to being a member of a profession. It is as important for a pastor to be as aware of the knowable aspects of self as it is for the physician to keep up on the latest drugs or a lawyer to know recent court rulings.

An excellent opportunity for gaining this kind of self-knowledge can be found in the kind of experience that is variously labeled *sensitivity training*, T-group, training laboratory, or human relations training. This involves intensive group interaction in which individuals are as open and honest with one another as they can be. Contrary to some unfortunate publicity sensitivity training has received, it is not "brain washing" or nude "swim-ins." Properly conducted, sensitivity training experience can be extremely helpful to the pastor in his interpersonal relationships.[9]

Being One's Self

It is not enough merely to acknowledge his inner experiences. The pastor also needs to *be* what he is. This is where the second part of the problem, the part created by being a Christian, becomes acute.

Many of the things that a pastor is by nature are not what the pastoral role requires. He is forced by his Christian commitment and his position as pastor to assume ill-fitting roles. For example, he can't tell the congregation chairman what he really thinks of him. He has to restrain his temper, his avarice, his impulses to vulgarity and profanity, or whatever his particular temptations are. Some have suggested that the pastor ought to go ahead and be what he is even in these ways. They believe that this would bring a whole new era of forthrightness and honesty to the church. This, they say, would transform the church. Contrary to what might be expected, they think, it would strengthen and revitalize the church rather than weaken and besmirch it.

It is difficult to imagine pastors acting out all their impulses. A more moderate alternative seems to be this: the pastor needs to be himself as much as he can without bringing offense to the Gospel, which he represents. There are large areas of role-playing in which the pastor is tempted to be something he is not that do not involve Christian morality at all. For example, the pastor may be tempted to deny his mistakes rather than acknowledge them. Such behavior is unfortunate because it usually stems from the notion that admission of mistakes will somehow degrade one in the eyes of others. In fact it does not, and in most instances it strengthens one because of its basic honesty. In similar ways, the pastor may be tempted to effect a manner of speech (big words, slang, an accent) or what he imagines is a profound and impressive posture. He may pretend to be moved with grief at a funeral, with happiness at a wedding, with joy at someone else's good fortune, when in fact he feels little emotional reaction. He may be tempted to pretend he knows the answers to everything. How much better if the pastor is just himself!

In addition to being himself as much as possible in non-moral matters, the pastor has to cope with the truly moral aspects of himself. Here he cannot merely be what he is, even though he ought to be well acquainted with himself. Here he has to strive to be God's kind of man, more like Christ. But his sinful nature works against that goal. The only way he can bring his real self into better line with what he ought to be is by growing in Christian grace and virtue (more about this in a moment).

Communicating One's Involvement

While this growth is going on, and since it cannot be perfected in this life, the kind of image of himself that the pastor presents to others is crucial. The pastor needs to act and talk and preach in such a way that he communicates to people his own involvement in the human condition. Then his people know he is human. They know he can feel what they feel. They know he can be empathic and understanding and that he can experience something of their lives.

How to tell a pastor when he is or is not communicating his own involvement in the human predicament is not easy. It can be a matter of choice of words, talking about "we sinners" rather than "you sinners." But it is more than words. Some pastors always say "we" and never "you," yet the parishioner reads him as saying "you." The self-inclusion does not come through because it is not really there.

It finally comes down to a matter of inner attitude. The pastor needs to talk and act and preach according to what he knows of the human condition from what he has learned as he has evaluated himself in the light of God's Word. Then he can communicate by word and gesture, by facial expression and tone of voice, that he knows what the human situation is. He knows because he is caught in it too, and he is struggling just as his people are struggling. People don't want him to condone sin. They just want him to acknowledge that it exists, that it is hard to handle. They want to know that he will still accept them in spite of what they are.

The Pastor's Own Faith and His Use of the Word

By far the most important issue of all for the pastor as a person is his own faith and his own use of the Word of God.

We said above that the pastor understands his own involvement in the human situation by examining himself in the light of God's Word. He finds, of course, that he falls far short of what he should be. He does what he shouldn't do; he fails to do what he should do. He lacks in those qualities of patience, love, charity, and understanding that are vital for a minister of the Word and, of course, for a counselor. Therefore he must grow, as we said, in Christian grace and virtue.

But how does he do that? God's law tells him only how and why he is in trouble, what the problem is. The Word of God works conviction about sin. The result is a *Yes!* to conscience and a *Yes!* to God's judgment. But up to that point he is only in difficulty. Something much greater is needed.

That something is the Gospel, which tells him about the saving work of God in Christ. It is on that Gospel that the pastor hangs his faith-hope. For it is by that message regarding Christ's life, death, and resurrection that the Holy Spirit creates and maintains faith.

It is absolutely essential that the pastor keep in constant contact with the Gospel. He keeps contact through his private study of the Word. He keeps contact through the very acts of communicating the message to others—through preaching, teaching, speaking, and discussing the Word. He is not merely addressing the message to others; he is also listening to and absorbing the message himself. He keeps contact through his own participation in the Holy Eucharist. For Word and sacrament are the means by which the Spirit comes among men and enables them to grow in godliness and virtue. Ultimately, as a result, the pastor's filling of the role of servant of men and exemplar of the faith becomes less and less put on. It becomes more and more an integral part of his person, of his whole being. It becomes more and more genuine and natural for him to be God's kind of man. He is then not "playing" a role. *He is the role.*

This growth in Christian faith and life has implications for both counseling and pastoral care. It means, on the one hand, that the pastor will be communicating God's Word *explicitly*. In pastoral care he will bring in both Law and Gospel as the occasion demands. One time he may show a person how he stands before God in terms of sin and judgment. Another time he may point to the mercy and forgiveness of God. Still another time he may direct the individual to the ways he can respond with a life of service and help to others. While he will not be quite so direct or so quick in doing these things in counseling, he has not relinquished his right to bring them in. He responds to and *reflects* the individual's own religious concerns and ideas. He uses gentle *confrontation* when the person fails to relate himself to God's Word. He uses gentle *probing* to help the individual explore himself in the light of God's Word.

The pastor's growth in faith and Christian life will have another kind of effect too. He will communicate his own commitment, his own faith, and his own participation in the Christian life *implicitly*. Not everything that is said about faith and life, about judgment and forgiveness, about Law and Gospel has to be said in words. It can also be expressed by his manner, by his attitudes, by the way he presents himself, in short, by *the person he is*. In pastoral care and counseling his own sense of forgiveness, his own trust in the Lord, his own tolerance and empathic understanding point to the Christ who has permeated his life. They preach a wordless sermon.

The Challenge

The pastor meets countless people in distress of all kinds. Some he serves with preaching, teaching, and administration of the sacraments. Some he helps to meet an acute problem through pastoral care. To a small percentage he offers pastoral counseling. Some he refers to another profession or agency. But through it all his concern is for their spiritual welfare. By word and action, explicitly and implicitly, by direct and indirect means he conveys the Gospel of Jesus Christ. His task is never done . . .

> till we all come in the unity of the faith, and of the knowledge of the Son of God, unto a perfect man, unto the measure of the stature of the fullness of Christ. —*Ephesians 4:13*

Notes

1. To be distinguished from *functional* mental disorders, in which no physical cause for the disorder is known.

2. The most accessible treatment of unconscious processes by Freud himself is in *A General Introduction to Psychoanalysis,* which is available in several paperback editions. See Appendix.

3. M. Strommen, *Profiles of Church Youth* (St. Louis: Concordia Publishing House, 1963).

4. The following section draws on the sources by Rogers cited in the Appendix.

5. These response categories are based in part on those of E. H. Porter, *An Introduction to Therapeutic Counseling* (Boston: Houghton Mifflin, 1950).

6. Committee on Nomenclature and Statistics of the American Psychiatric Association. *Diagnostic and Statistical Manual.* 2d ed. (Washington: American Psychiatric Association, 1968).

7. One exception is severe alcoholism, where relatively good success is attained by Alcoholics Anonymous.

8. A truly excellent book on this topic is: H. Faber and E. van der Schoot, *The Art of Pastoral Conversation* (New York: Abingdon Press, 1965).

9. Programs conducted by National Training Laboratories in association with the National Education Association are particularly well supervised.

Suggested Readings

In line with the author's basic conviction that each individual must work out his own approach to counseling, the following suggestions for further reading are presented.

I. *Client-Centered Therapy*

To begin at the beginning, two volumes by Carl R. Rogers probably should be read:

Rogers, Carl R. *Counseling and Psychotherapy: Newer Concepts in Practice.* Boston: Houghton Mifflin, 1942.

– – –. *Client-Centered Therapy.* Boston: Houghton Mifflin, 1951.

But it may not be necessary to begin at the beginning. The following is a very readable volume that gives considerable insight into Rogers himself and his ideas about counseling and helping relationships. It is highly recommended.

Rogers, Carl R. *On Becoming a Person.* Boston: Houghton Mifflin, 1961.

A systematic statement by Rogers concerning his views on the nature of personality formation and how it can be altered, a must for the serious reader, is:

Rogers, Carl R. "A Theory of Therapy, Personality, and Interpersonal Relationships, as Developed in the Client-Centered Framework," *Psychology: a Study of a Science,* Vol. 3, *Formulations of the Person and the Social Context,* ed. Sigmund Koch. New York: McGraw-Hill, 1959.

A concise statement of the conditions Rogers believes are essential to any helping relationship, a statement heavily drawn upon in Chapter 2, should be read as a primary source:

Rogers, Carl R. "The Necessary and Sufficient Conditions of Therapeutic Personality Change," *Journal of Consulting Psychology,* XXI (1957), 95–103.

A statement of current trends and recent developments in client-centered thinking can be found in:

Seeman, J. "Perspectives in Client-Centered Therapy," *Handbook of Clinical Psychology,* ed. Benjamin B. Wolman. New York: Mc-Graw-Hill, 1965.

II. *Psychoanalysis*

The collected works of Freud will occupy some 24 volumes in translation:

Freud, Sigmund. *The Standard Edition of the Complete Psychological Works of Sigmund Freud.* New York: Macmillan, 1964.

Easily accessible in paperback are the following items:

Freud, Sigmund. *A General Introduction to Psychoanalysis.* New York: Washington Square Press.

— — —. *New Introductory Lectures on Psychoanalysis,* trans. James Strachey. New York: Norton, 1965.

— — —. *Outline of Psychoanalysis,* trans. James Strachey. New York: Norton, 1949.

Freud in the original is wordy and sometimes hard to grasp, and it is better to start with an overview like one of the following, although the reader owes it to himself to read at least some Freud to get the flavor of his writing and thinking.

Brenner, Charles. *Elementary Textbook of Psychoanalysis.* Garden City, New York: Doubleday Anchor Books, 1957.

Ross, N., and S. Abrams. "Fundamentals of Psychoanalytic Theory," *Handbook of Clinical Psychology,* ed. Benjamin B. Wolman. New York: McGraw-Hill, 1965.

The most comprehensive treatment of the life and work of Freud is:

Jones, Ernest. *The Life and Works of Sigmund Freud.* 3 vols. New York: Basic Books, 1953—57.

Recommended statements on psychoanalytic treatment per se that contain ideas that would be fruitful for the pastor-counselor are:

Alexander, Franz. *Fundamentals of Psychoanalysis.* New York: Norton, 1963. Paperback.

Fromm-Reichmann, Frieda. *Principles of Intensive Psychotherapy.* Chicago: University of Chicago Press, 1950. Paperback.

Menninger, Karl. *Theory of Psychoanalytic Technique.* New York: Harper & Row Torchbooks, 1964. Paperback.

There are many derivatives and offshoots of psychoanalysis, too many to be cited here, but an excellent examination of the major ones may be found in:

Munroe, Ruth L. *Schools of Psychoanalytic Thought.* New York: Holt, Rinehart and Winston, 1955.

A briefer treatment of related approaches is:

Mullahy, Patrick. "Non-Freudian Analytic Theories," *Handbook of Clinical Psychology,* ed. Benjamin B. Wolman. New York: McGraw-Hill, 1965.

III. *Rational and Persuasive Approaches*

Although not representative of the point of view of this book, the following approaches, which take the position of giving people the information they need to achieve sensible solutions to their problems and persuading them to adopt different attitudes and behavior patterns, are worthy of attention:

Ellis, Albert. *Reason and Emotion in Psychotherapy.* New York: Lyle Stuart, 1962.

Thorne, F. C. "Personality: a Clinical Eclectic Viewpoint." Brandon, Vt.: *Journal of Clinical Psychology,* 1961.

Williamson, Edmund G. *Vocational Counseling: Some Historical, Philosophical, and Theoretical Perspectives.* New York: McGraw-Hill, 1965.

IV. *Behavior Conditioning*

These approaches have little in common with "talking treatment" of the types considered above. Yet they promise to be a continuing major factor in the field of counseling and psychotherapy and may be of interest to the reader.

Eysenck, H. J., ed. *Behaviour Therapy and the Neuroses.* Oxford: Pergamon Press, 1960.

Wolpe, Joseph, and Arnold A. Lazarus. *Behavior Therapy Techniques: A Guide to the Treatment of Neuroses.* Oxford: Pergamon Press, 1966.

Wolpe, Joseph, A. Salter, and L. J. Reyna. *The Conditioning Therapies.* New York: Holt, Rinehart and Winston, 1964.

Pastoral Counseling with People in Distress

Harold J. Haas

The pastor is often the first, and perhaps only, professional person to whom people in distress go for comfort and counsel. For some of these situations the pastor requires additional training and study in counseling people with mental and emotional problems.

In this book an experienced pastor and practicing clinical psychologist presents a basic outline on mental and emotional problems and basic counseling concepts especially for pastors. In the preface Dr. Haas states that what pastors need is "a point of view about how to meet people in trouble and a reasonably concrete set of ideas about the methods they can use in counseling. They also need some signposts that will tell them when a problem is beyond their competency so they can make appropriate referrals to other members of the mental health team. I have tried to meet these needs in this volume."

In suggesting an approach to people in distress, Dr. Haas distinguishes between emotional distress and mental disorder, then describes the various mental health professions and their approaches to therapy. These mental health workers share certain goals with the pastor: to alleviate emotional distress and to help a person fulfill his potential as a human